303

NEW LIGHT ON ANCIENT CARTHAGE

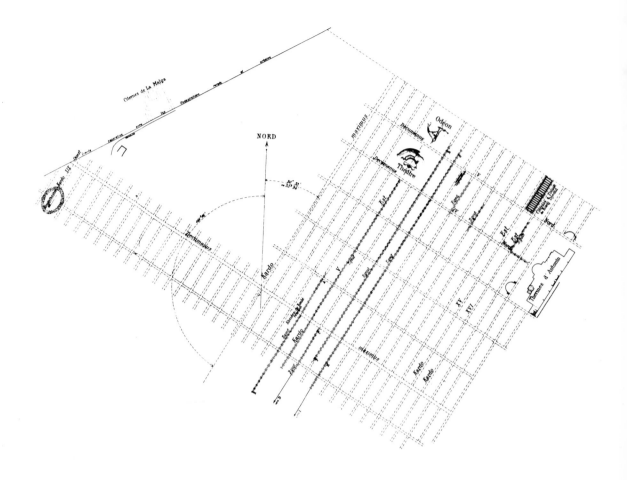

Plan of Roman Carthage. (*Courtesy of The MIT Press.*)

NEW LIGHT ON ANCIENT CARTHAGE

Edited by John Griffiths Pedley

Papers of a Symposium Sponsored by
the Kelsey Museum of Archaeology,
the University of Michigan,
Marking the Fiftieth Anniversary of the Museum

ANN ARBOR   THE UNIVERSITY OF MICHIGAN PRESS

Frontispiece reprinted from fig. 50, *Orthogonal Town Planning in Antiquity,* by Ferdinando Castagnoli. Reprinted by permission of The MIT Press.

Library of Congress Cataloging in Publication Data
Main entry under title:

New light on ancient Carthage.

Bibliography: p.
1. Carthage—Antiquities—Congresses. 2. Carthage—History—Congresses. I. Pedley, John Griffiths.
II. Michigan. University. Kelsey Museum of Archaeology.
DT269.C33N48   939'.73   80–16536
ISBN 0–472–10003–3

Foreword

An archaeological campaign, initiated by the United Nations Educational, Scientific, and Cultural Organization (UNESCO) in 1972, has been conducted for several years at Carthage. Its purpose is manifold: to save a prestigious site from a threatening urbanization, to bring to light remains testifying to its richness, and to preserve and restore the discovered monuments and documents—in short, to better reveal the history of the civilization that developed in the territory of this city.

Teams of experts from many countries have therefore undertaken important archaeological researches within the framework of this great international campaign. The United States, under the auspices of the American Schools of Oriental Research (ASOR) project, has sent two teams, one under the direction of Lawrence E. Stager for the Punic period, the other under the direction of John Humphrey for the Roman period.

To be sure, to the minds of those responsible the urgent priority was the protection of the site against the encroaching town development, and this was the major reason for the initiation of this international campaign. The extensive international excavations that have been undertaken have indeed played an essential role in halting the destruction of the site, in revealing the importance and richness of its archaeological heritage. Yet at the same time as they uncovered and progressively restored this heritage, these archaeological teams have had a considerable effect in the scientific sphere: their investigations are in the process of renovating the whole history of ancient Carthage in establishing its solid foundations.

This revival of a scientific interest in the history of Carthage is, indeed, one of the most important consequences of the International Preservation Campaign. It is the privilege of the excavators of the new international generation to have come to Carthage, to have taken part in the recovery of its history, to have brought to light, with method and patience, a multitude of discoveries and observations. It will be also to their merit to have safeguarded, studied, and made known the results of their research by bringing them to the growing attention of the public.

In this regard, the two ASOR teams are pioneers. They have not only participated actively in the field and worked for the preservation of the site, but also published their first results. Even better, they have organized, on the occasion of the fiftieth anniversary of the foundation of the Kelsey Museum, an exhibition called "Carthage Then and Now," and, on this favorable occasion, held a colloquium on Carthage.

This was a modest symposium, to be sure, since it was restricted to scholars of the New World and a few visiting experts, but significant in its import. For it testifies to the interest in America in these investigations, as well as to the quality of the participants. This volume, the result of the symposium held in Ann Arbor on March 23 and 24, 1979, is composed of seven solid, unpublished studies all dealing with Carthage. One cannot congratulate too much Messrs. Wright, Cross, and King, presidents of the American Schools of Oriental Research, who, with their collaborators, were the instigators and sponsors of all the American activity on behalf of Carthage, and Mr. Pedley, who kept an eye on its organization and was instrumental in bringing it to a successful conclusion. Nor can one thank too much all the scholars, as well as their teams, for these contributions that testify to the revival of studies on Carthage. Here is an outstanding contribution in support of the preservation of Carthage.

Abdelmajid Ennabli
Curator of the Site of Carthage

Preface

In 1925 the University of Michigan took part in excavations at Carthage in cooperation with a team of French archaeologists and under the enthusiastic leadership of Professor F. W. Kelsey. Professor Kelsey, professor of Latin literature and language at the University from 1889 to 1927, was a dominant figure in archaeological circles in the United States for much of his life, and was a devotee of antiquities and publication as witness the long series of volumes edited by him between 1904 and 1927 in the Michigan Humanistic Series, and the collections of Roman materials that he began to bring together in Ann Arbor. It is these materials that form the basis of the Kelsey Museum's collections, and that made necessary the provision by the University authorities of a museum to hold, study, preserve, and publish them. The museum itself did not open its doors to the public until 1929, lamentably two years after Professor Kelsey's death, but there can be no doubt that his plans called for the purchase or construction of such a building, and that the museum is rightly named after this majestic pioneer.

Although in 1925 the *New York Times* was already commenting on the negative aspects of twentieth-century urbanization with respect to Carthage, a concerted attempt to unravel the history and archaeology of the city had to await the inspired initiative in 1972 of the Tunisian Institute of Art and Archaeology. Under the auspices of UNESCO, the Tunisian Institute in that year appealed for an international effort to recover the remains of the ancient city before it was too late. With the example of Aswan before them, foreign teams were quickly in the field: Poland, Bulgaria, Britain, Italy, France, Germany, Denmark, Canada, and the United States have all in recent years sent highly qualified teams to work on different aspects and in different areas of the ancient city. Tunisia herself, of course, also has had an energetic and eminently successful team at work. It is a spectacular example of corroborative and cooperative work being carried out with diverse methods in diverse chronological ranges with exceptional success and there can be no doubt that the work has been and is being done just in time. Equally there can be no doubt that without the urgent prompting and skillful coordination of the Tunisian Institute, a coherent picture of ancient Carthage would have been lost. It has been a rare privilege for the Kelsey Museum—under the auspices of the American Schools of Oriental Research—to have provided one of the teams from the United States to play a part in this remarkable research.

In celebrating the fiftieth anniversary of the Kelsey Museum in 1979, two projects have accordingly seemed most appropriate. First, an exhibition linking the work of Kelsey's team in the twenties with the museum's more recent activities in Carthage, "Carthage Then and Now" (January 26 to July 31, 1979); second, a symposium held in Ann Arbor on March 23 and 24, 1979, bringing together leading participants in the current work in Carthage, the papers of which are published here.

Current pervasive funding problems compelled the museum to restrict participation to Carthaginian colleagues in North America, and it was our singular good fortune to find Professor Serge Lancel of the University of Grenoble, director of the French excavations, at the Institute for Advanced Study in Princeton this year. For taking time from a richly deserved sabbatical leave to share in our celebrations, the museum is most grateful to him, as indeed we are to all our Canadian colleagues and friends from Chicago whose names appear on the contents page: to Professor Pierre Senay, of the University of Quebec at Trois Rivières, principal investigator of the first Canadian team; to Professor Colin Wells of the University of Ottawa and Professor Edith Wightman of McMaster University, principal investigators of the second Canadian team; to Professor Katherine Dunbabin also of McMaster University and Dr. John Hayes of the Royal Ontario Museum, both active participants in the current work in Carthage and much in demand for their expertise in pavements and pottery; and to Professor Lawrence E. Stager of the Oriental Institute of the University of Chicago, field director of the other American team in Carthage. To them all, our warmest thanks. I would like to add a personal note of thanks to Professor John Humphrey, of the staff of the museum, not only for contributing his paper but also for his devotion to and direction of the Michigan work at Carthage. For unfailing help with the many details that go to make a symposium successful, I am happy to record a great debt of gratitude to all members of the museum staff, and especially to Kathy Font and David Slee.

The major debt of gratitude, however, is owed, and happily acknowledged, to Dr. Azzedine Beschaousch, Director of the Tunisian Institute of Art and Archaeology, and to Dr. Abdelmajid Ennabli, Curator of the Site of Carthage and coordinator of the whole international operation. They not only inaugurated and encouraged the research, but also allowed the contributors to the symposium to use new materials and new ideas, and permitted the publication of the papers. All publications relating to the new excavations are under the auspices of UNESCO and within the framework of the Advisory Committee of Tunisia.

I hope the perusal of these essays will bring the reader as much pleasure and profit as it has given me, and that the volume will prove a worthy emblem with which to mark the fifitieth anniversary of the museum.

John Griffiths Pedley
Director, Kelsey Museum of Archaeology
University of Michigan

Contents

Abbreviations

AJA—American Journal of Archaeology

AJP—American Journal of Philology

AntAfr—Antiquités Africaines

AntJ—Antiquaries' Journal

BAC—Bulletin archéologique du Comité des travaux historiques et archéologiques

BCH—Bulletin de correspondance hellenique

BSAF—Bulletin de la Societé des Antiquaires de France

CEDAC—Centre d'Études et de Documentation Archéologique de la conservation de Carthage

CIL—Corpus Inscriptionum Latinarum

CIS—Corpus Inscriptionum Semiticarum

CR—Classical Review

CRAI—Comptes rendus de l'Académie des inscriptions et belles lettres

CSEL—Corpus Scriptorum Ecclesiae Latinorum

DOPapers—Dumbarton Oaks Papers

EMC/CNV—Echos du monde classique/Classical News and Views

FGrH—Jacoby, *Fragmente der griechischen Historiker*

FIRA—Fontes Iuris Romani AnteJustiniani

HAAN—Gsell, *Histoire ancienne de l'Afrique du Nord* (Paris, 1913)

InvTun—Gauckler, *Inventaire des Mosaiques de la Gaule et de l'Afrique II, Afrique Proconsulaire,* (Tunisie) (Paris, 1910)

JFA—Journal of Field Archaeology

JRS—Journal of Roman Studies

JSav—Journal des Savants

MelRome—Mélanges d'archéologie et d'histoire de l'Ecole francaise de Rome

MelRomeA—Mélanges de l'Ecole francaise de Rome: Antiquités

MonPiot—Monuments et memoires publ. par l'Académie des inscriptions et belles lettres, Fondation Piot.

NouvArch—Nouvelles archives des missions scientifiques

PSAM—Publications du Service des Antiquités de Maroc

RA—Revue archéologique

RAfr—Revue africaine

RE—Pauly-Wissowa, *Real-Encyclopädie der klassischen Altertumwissenschaft*

RevPhil—Revue de philologie, de litterature, et de l'histoire anciennes
RevTun—Revue Tunisienne
RHist—Revue historique
RomMitt—Mitteilungen des deutschen archaologischen Instituts, Römische Ab-
    teilung.

I. The Rite of Child Sacrifice at Carthage

Lawrence E. Stager

Lawrence E. Stager

INTRODUCTION TO THE PRECINCT OF TANIT, NOW CALLED TOPHET

In the closing weeks of 1921, François Icard uncovered evidence of a Punic sanctuary some fifty meters west of a shallow lagoon (now known to be the site of the Punic Commercial Port). These remains consisted primarily of layers of stelae and urns, the latter containing the bones "probably of animals."[1] Icard's initial impression was soon corrected by Dr. P. Pallary, who examined the contents of more than eighty urns and found the bones to be those of children, with some sheep-goat and birds also represented.[2]

By early 1922, Louis Poinssot and Raymond Lantier had assumed, or usurped, control of these early excavations, although Icard and his partner Gielly remained in charge of day-to-day operations. In 1925 a joint Franco-American expedition under the direction of Francis Kelsey of the University of Michigan continued excavations begun in the previous year by the Count de Prorok.[3] Kelsey's death in 1926 brought that expedition to a halt (fig. 1-1). Between 1934 and 1936 Père Lapeyre directed further digging in the precinct.[4] And Pierre Cintas directed yet another round of excavation in the mid-1940s.[5]

The problem of the precinct has not been lack of digging (thousands of urns and monuments have been removed), but rather the failure to publish the results fully and systematically. Poinssot and Lantier's preliminary report on the earliest excavations[6] has yet to be matched in promptness of publication and breadth of coverage, although even that study was incomplete in itself and was never followed by a full final report. Harden's pioneering study of the urns from Kelsey's excavations established a pottery typology and chronology for Carthage that still remains generally valid. For this urn sequence Harden relied more on the seriation of tomb pottery than on the rather gross stratigraphy provided by Kelsey's single season of excavations in the Tophet.[7]

STRATIGRAPHY AND CHRONOLOGY

Icard (1922) detected four strata in the precinct: A (700–500 B.C.), B (500–400 B.C.), C (400–300 B.C.), and D (300–146 B.C.).[8] Yet Harden, after Kelsey's work in almost the same area, was willing to isolate only three strata: Tanit I (800 to early seventh century B.C.), Tanit II (early seventh to late fourth century B.C.), and Tanit III (late fourth century to 146 B.C.).[9]

Our excavations have produced stratigraphic evidence for suggesting at least eight phases of urn burials. Each phase represents a new level from which urn pits were dug. However, only in area 1 were all eight phases found superimposed. Phases I through IV have Tanit I-type urns, usually decorated with wide red-slipped and burnished bands at the waist and vertical line groups (triglyph-metope pattern) at the shoulder (figs. 1-2 and 1-3). Phases V through VIII belong to the Tanit II period. Most of the two-handled, wasp-waisted urns in buff to yellow clay date to phases VII through VIII (fourth century B.C. and later?). The Romans left practically nothing in situ from the Tanit III horizon. Except for a general phase IX, we have no clear indication of how many additional phases of urn burial there might have been in Tanit III. The urns are smaller and even more standardized than in the late Tanit II period. I would tentatively date the urn sequence from about 700 B.C. to 146 B.C.[10]

The monuments (stelae and cippi) set up to mark the urns also underwent changes through time. Earlier excavators have reported that stone "cairns" served as markers for the earliest urns (Tanit I). Supposedly the urn was placed on bedrock and then covered with a pile of cobbles. The earliest urns we have found (phase I) were placed in pits dug into a matrix of black clay, about 0.25 meter thick, which rested on bedrock (caliche). The pits were lined with cobbles and capped with stones. The black clay deposit is natural—created when a large marsh dried up—and precedes the use of the precinct. If the prehistoric marsh sediments were mistakenly excavated first, leaving the stone lining of the pit exposed and freestanding, this might give the appearance of a cairn. In phases II and III small L-shaped cippi made of sandstone marked some of the Tanit I-type urns (fig. 1–4). Stelae first appear in phases VII through VIII. Made of micritic limestone, they have gables and sometimes incised inscriptions (fig. 1–5). By phase IX and later (Tanit III) the stelae of micritic limestone become much thinner and have gables flanked by *acroteria* (these are incipient on some of the thick stelae from phases VII through VIII).

NATURE AND USE OF PRECINCT

Some scholars, skeptical of the notion that child sacrifice was practiced systematically among the Canaanites, Israelites, and Phoenicians, have argued that the Carthaginians sacrificed their children only "sporadically" and in a form of "noninstitutionalized worship." Claude Schaeffer has argued that the precinct was not the site of ritual sacrifice, but simply a cemetery for infants and children who had died of natural causes;[11] in this, he has been followed by Moshe Weinfeld.[12] But the evidence—archaeological, epigraphic, and historical—points to the contrary.

The Carthaginian precinct shares with other infant burial grounds in the western Mediterranean the characteristics of being an open-air enclosure surrounded by a wall that sets it apart from other areas of the city. Our excavations have exposed a cut in bedrock, over 2.00 meters wide, indicating where the precinct's eastern wall had been standing before stone robbers dismantled it. In the Late Punic period, this wall separated the precinct from the quayside of the Commercial Harbor—the waterfront was just 45 meters to the east. Inside the wall we have recovered over 400 urns filled with charred human and animal bones set in pits dug into strata dating from around 700 to 146 B.C. The majority of urns we have excavated date to the fourth century B.C. when the density of burials was much higher than at any earlier period and the precinct reached its greatest extent. A *minimal* estimate for the size of the precinct in the fourth (and probably third) century B.C. is 5,000–6,000 square meters. Extrapolating from the density of urns in our excavated area, I should estimate that perhaps as many as 20,000 urns were deposited during 400–200 B.C. This would average out at 100 urn deposits per year, or slightly fewer than 1 every three days. Of course, we have no clear indication of the interval between interments, but the evidence is enough to suggest that the deposits were not a casual or sporadic occurrence.

The Greek and Roman writers give a variety of occasions when the Carthaginians practiced the rite of human sacrifice. These can be summarized as: regularly on an annual basis, in times of great crisis, and whenever "great favors" were requested from the gods. Diodorus records that as many as 500 children were sacrificed in Carthage's political crisis of 310 B.C.

> There was in their city a bronze image of Cronus, extending its hands, palms up and sloping toward the ground, so that each of the children when placed thereupon rolled down and fell into a sort of gaping pit filled with fire.[13]

At that time Carthage was being threatened by Agathocles, the ruler of Syracuse, who had landed on nearby Cap Bon with a large invasionary force. Diodorus, probably deriving from Timaeus of Tauromenium, records that such a mass sacrifice was expected to appease the gods and ward off the threat to Carthage.

The typical pattern we have found is the careful placement of usually one, sometimes two, and rarely three or more urns in a single pit, with no evidence so far for mass burials. Apart from their main contents, the calcined bones of humans or animals, some of the urns had offerings of amulets and beads once strung as necklaces (fig. 1–6). Generally the urns were sealed with red or yellow clay and capped with inverted bowls or dish-shaped lids. Urn stoppers were made of unbaked clay, probably taken from the same source as that used for the fired pottery urns. In the early period (Group A) red clay was used for both urn and stopper; later (Group B) yellow clay was predominant.

Infant corpses are composed of a high percentage of cartilage which is destroyed during cremation and so only the more completely ossified bones survive, such as the petrosals, cranial fragments, long bones, and phalanges. Teeth are the most heat resistant and the stage of dental development provides the most important criteria for determining the approximate age of the sacrificial victim. Unfortunately the sex of such young individuals cannot be determined from the osteological remains. The skeletal evidence that has been preserved indicates that a conscious effort was made by parents and/or priests to collect from the pyre or altar the particular remains of one or two individuals and deposit them in an urn.[14] This also argues against mass sacrifice since such concern for the identity of individual victims would not have been likely in the situation described by Diodorus. At the present time, the contents of 130 of the more than 400 urns have been studied preliminarily by Dr. Jeffrey Schwartz. Of this sample, 50 urns belong to the late Group B (fourth century B.C.) and 80 to the early Group A (mainly seventh century B.C.).

If the population profile for these two groups is sustained by further analyses, the contrasts between the practices of the seventh and fourth centuries B.C. are striking and useful not only for the changes in the cult itself but also for the comparative demographic picture of Carthage as a whole.

Group B has a high proportion of human to animal remains, approximately nine to one (table 1). Nearly 68 percent (30) of the urns with humans only contained the remains of a single child, usually between the ages of one and three years old. Premature or newborn infants make up

TABLE 1

Comparison of Human and Animal Remains from the Carthage Precinct, by Percentage and Number of Urns

	Human		Animal		Human plus Animal		
	%	Urns	%	Urns	%	Urns	Total Urns
Group A: seventh and sixth centuries B.C.	62.5	50	30	24	7.5	6	80
Group B: fourth century B.C.	88	44	10	5	2	1	50

Note: Of the more than 300 urns awaiting analysis, most belong to Group B.

30 percent of the single interment category. Surprisingly, about 32 percent of the urns of the fourth century B.C. contained two or three children. In the latter cases (triple interments), the dental morphology indicates that two of the three children were twins. So we shall speak of this category as double, or paired, interments, which invariably include a very young infant (or twins), either premature or neonatal, and a more mature child, two to four years old.

When inscribed stelae were set up to mark the urn burials, they recorded the genealogy (often at some length) of the dedicants who made the vow to Baʿal Ḥamon and Tanit. Not all of the urns were marked by such tombstones but when they were, it seems most likely that the dedicants were the parents of the interred child or children found in association with the stone. In this context the osteological data for double, or paired, interments in an urn raise interesting questions. A reasonable assumption when two individuals were buried in a single urn is that they were from the same family. If this is correct, it creates some insurmountable problems for those biblical scholars who have linked the Semitic practice of child sacrifice with the biblical Law of the First-born. According to Ezekiel 20:26, Yahweh declares:

> I defied them through their very gifts in making them offer by fire their first-born, that I might horrify them.

These injunctions suggest that the oldest son was "given" to Yahweh (see also Exod. 22:29b; 34:19–20).

The double interment usually contained a premature-neonatal individual plus a two to four year old. The age difference also supports the suggestion that both were from the same family since two years is the natural birth interval that can be expected in families not practicing prenatal forms of birth control. A possible explanation for the double interments arises from the description given by Kleitarchos (FGrH 137 F 9) in the third century B.C.:

> Out of reverence for Kronos (Baʿal Ḥamon), the Phoenicians, and especially the Carthaginians, whenever they seek to obtain some great favor, vow one of their children, burning it as a sacrifice to the deity, if they are especially eager to gain success.[15]

It is in terms of the vow (Phoenician/Punic *ndr*, which frequently occurs on inscribed stelae) made by the parents of the sacrificed children that we should attempt to interpret the double interments. We can imagine a scenario somewhat as follows:

> In fulfillment of a vow for a favor granted (or to be granted) by the deity, the parent pledges his unborn child. But this child is either born dead or dies before the time of sacrifice (the premature-neonatal individual). To fulfill the vow the parent is obliged to sacrifice the youngest living offspring (the two to four year old) as an acceptable response to the favor granted (or to be granted) by the god.[16]

Dr. Paul Mosca has recently reassessed sacrificial terms that appear on inscribed stelae from Carthage and from other sites in the Mediterranean. He found that some of these terms, particularly those involving *mulk*-sacrifices, could definitely be related to Tophet rites. The word *mlk* (*mulk*) appears in the Bible in contexts that involved sacrificial rites on the "high places of Tophet" in a valley just outside Jerusalem. There "sons and daughters" were made to "pass through the fire to Molek" (Jer. 32:35; 2 Kings 23:10). Probably the word *Molek* should be revocalized and read as *mulk,* a particular kind of sacrifice. At Carthage only two types of *mulk*-sacrifice are attested in the stelae inscriptions: *mulk ʾimmōr**, the sacrifice of a lamb or a kid, and *mulk baʿal,* the sacrifice of a "baʿal," namely the child of a wealthy mercantile or estate-owning family. Mosca contrasts the latter type with the *mulk ʾadam,* sacrifice of a commoner, a term that appears at other sites in the second century B.C., but remains unattested at Carthage. These two terms may reflect a basic social stratification in Punic society between the upper class (estate-owners and merchants) and the proletariat (peasants, for example).[17]

Thus it appears from these difficult technical terms that many of the elite families were sacrificing their children in the Tophet rites at Carthage. In the few instances where the vocation of the offerant is actually noted on the stelae, these also support the notion that at Carthage the elite were among the most active participants in the rite. From our excavations there is little doubt that monuments in their original position can be related to a particular urn. Usually the stelae or cippi were placed directly above the urn to mark the burial of the sacrifice. However, not every urn has a marker that can be associated with it. Do these sacrifices represent those of commoners who could not afford tombstones or do they indicate instances in which monuments have been plucked and then reused in later burials (of which there are a number of examples) or simply removed for other reasons?

Some Carthaginians were apparently allowed, or chose, to offer animals such as sheep or goats as an acceptable substitute. In both the seventh and fourth centuries B.C. some urns contained *only* the calcined remains of young sheep or goats. When sex could be determined, the lambs and kids were males. It seems that either sheep or goat was included in the *mulk ' immōr** sacrifice. In one case an L-shaped sandstone cippus marked an urn burial containing only charred sheep bones (fig. 1–7).

Although these child sacrifices were performed in a religious context and viewed by the Carthaginian elite from that perspective, the rite most probably also had practical benefits for these wealthy families. They could use this institution as a mechanism for regulating their growth and maintaining their socioeconomic status. Perhaps as an example, partible inheritance such as the large estates in and around Carthage could be passed on for generations without being greatly subdivided, thus maintaining the wealth and power of the proprietary family. As Carthage grew to metropolitan proportions in the fourth century B.C., this "hidden logic" to child sacrifice now becomes more apparent.

In the early sample (Group A), the percentage of sheep-goat victims is much higher (30 percent [24 urns]) than in the later period (10 percent [5 urns]). This figure is in keeping with Pallary's findings of 1922 and in opposition to the results of Richard,[18] who concluded that there was a steady increase in animal substitution and thus an attenuation of child sacrifice with the passage of time. But his sample was small (42 urns from Carthage) and included urns from Sousse-Hadrumetum.

The "human only" category of Group A urns was also different from that of Group B. The human sacrifices of the seventh century B.C. were usually very young—premature or newborn infants. The fourth century B.C. victims included newborns but an even greater number of children one year and older.

Several Phoenician colonies in the western Mediterranean have precincts of child sacrifice that date to the early periods of the founding settlement (e.g., Motya, Sicily; Tharros and Sulcis, Sardinia; and Carthage, Tunisia; whereas the early Phoenician foundations in Spain have produced no evidence for child sacrifice). Why such an institution, with potentially dire consequences for a fledgling colony, should have been established at such an early date has intrigued but puzzled me for years.

It is not difficult to imagine what a complete disaster Jamestown, Virginia, would have been had the founders been sacrificing children. Only 60 of 500 colonists survived the horrible winter of 1609–10; to avoid starving, some resorted to cannibalism. And even after a decade in Jamestown, the colonists were still largely dependent upon the Indians for food.[19]

But historical analogies of this sort are to some degree misleading. The ecological hardships suffered by Phoenician founders were hardly so extreme as those encountered by European colonists settling in the New World. The coastal zones of the Mediterranean have a great deal in common, so much so that the Phoenicians tended to settle on coast lines similar to those of the homeland. But even under the most favorable conditions, it would not have been an easy task to keep a young colony going and growing if child sacrifice were widespread and frequent. Such religious ideology would have soon thwarted other attempts toward growth. Unless there were a continual influx of newcomers from the motherland (which seems unlikely), the institution of child sacrifice coupled with colonial mortality rates (which must have been higher for both infants and adults even under the best of circumstances) would have proved suicidal for many of the colonies.

Self-extinction was not the purpose or the consequence of child sacrifice at Carthage, where the practice persisted for more than five centuries. I believe that one of the primary reasons the rite did not result in such a predicament was due to the flexibility provided by the option of animal substitution. Sacrificing an animal in place of a child was an acceptable custom from the earliest days of the West Phoenician colonies. A seventh century B.C. inscription from Malta mentions the *mlk 'mr*.[20] At Carthage there is inscriptional evidence for this type of Tophet sacrifice in the third century B.C.[21] Sheep are depicted on some limestone stelae from the fourth century B.C. to 146 B.C. The Latin transcription *molchomor* for the Phoenician technical term *mulk 'immōr** is attested in the Ngaous stelae (Algeria) in the second and third centuries A.D. There the meaning is made clear by the telling phrase *agnum pro vika(rio)*.[22]

Animal substitution provided the optional means by which an otherwise rigid sacrificial system could adapt to, in fact reinforce, the changing demographic situations of the colony. In the early days of Carthage animal substitution was widely accepted as an appropriate response to the imperative for Tophet sacrifices. Later on in the fourth through third centuries B.C., when New Carthage was being developed along the shorelines of the Gulf of Tunis[23] and the metropolitan area probably exceeded a quarter million people, animal substitution was not a common practice in Tophet rites. At that time children, not animals, were by far the most common sacrificial victims. In this way the elite could control their numbers in a rather systematic way while still receiving the blessings of the gods.

From this analysis, which of course remains tentative until all of the urn contents have been studied, I have difficulty accepting the evolutionary scheme proposed by many historians of religion and cultural evolutionists who maintain that the "barbaric" practice of human sacrifice was gradually replaced by the more "civilized" practice of animal substitution. Abraham substituting the "ram-in-the-thicket" for his son Isaac is usually considered paradigmatic. Such was not the case in Carthage: it is precisely in the fourth through third centuries B.C., when Carthage had attained the heights of urbanity, that child sacrifice flourished as never before.

NOTES

My essay is built on contributions from and discussion with several staff members of the Punic Project. In the field, Douglas Esse, Joseph Greene, and Samuel Wolff, all Ph.D. candidates in Near Eastern archaeology at the University of Chicago, personally excavated most of the urn burials; no local labor was used because of the delicacy of the operations. Their recognition of the various ground levels from which urn pits were dug (and their meticulous recording of the details) provided the essential stratigraphic information for unraveling the incredibly complicated sequence of burial phases in the Tophet. During seven months of field work in area 1, Esse removed thirty cubic meters of soil and discovered over 200 urns.

Dr. Paul Mosca, staff epigraphist from the University of British Columbia, established many of the intellectual parameters of the project with his treatment of the classical and inscriptional sources in "Child Sacrifice in Canaanite and Israelite Religion" (1975), a Harvard doctoral dissertation, under the direction of our principal investigator, Frank M. Cross.

Many of the most important contributions to understanding Carthaginian child sacrifice have come from the analyses of urn contents by Dr. Jeffrey Schwartz, staff osteologist from the University of Pittsburgh. He has painstakingly assessed the often very fragmentary remains of calcined bones found in each excavated urn and is providing the first systematic study of datable urn contents. When completed, his analyses will provide a wealth of data for future interpretations of the rite of child sacrifice.

I bear sole responsibility for the present, possibly premature, interpretation of the evidence that attempts to explain how the institution functioned in terms of demography.

1. F. Icard, "Séance de la Commission de l'Afrique du Nord," *Bulletin archéologique,* 1922, pp. 23–24, 42–45.

2. P. Pallary, "Note sur les urnes funéraires trouvées à Salammbô près Carthage," *Revue Tunisienne* 152–54 (1922): 206–11.

3. D. B. Harden, "Punic Urns from the Precinct of Tanit at Carthage," *AJA* 31 (1927): 297–310; idem, "The Pottery from the Precinct of Tanit at Salammbô, Carthage," *Iraq* 4 (1937): 59–89; F. W. Kelsey, *Excavations at Carthage, 1925: A Preliminary Report* (New York, 1926).

4. R. P. Lapeyre, "Fouilles récéntes à Carthage," *CRAI,* 1935, pp. 81–87; idem, "Les fouilles du Musée Lavigerie à Carthage de 1935 a 1939. I. Temple de Tanit," *CRAI,* 1939, pp. 294–300.

5. P. Cintas, *Manuel d'archéologie punique* (Paris, 1970), 1: 311–429; G. Picard, "Le sanctuaire dit de Tanit à Carthage," *CRAI,* 1945, pp. 443–52.

6. L. Poinssot and R. Lantier, "Un Sanctuaire de Tanit à Carthage," *Revue de l'histoire des religions* 87 (1923): 32–68.

7. For a more complete discussion of the history of the excavations in the Precinct of Tanit, see P. G. Mosca, "Child Sacrifice in Canaanite and Israelite Religion: A Study in *Mulk* and מלך " (Ph.D. thesis, Harvard University, 1975). P. G. Mosca, J. H. Schwartz, and L. E. Stager, "The Sanctuary: A Summary," in *Carthage Excavations, 1976–77: Punic Project, Second Interim Report,* ed. L. E. Stager (Chicago, in press).

8. For the dates, see Poinssot and Lantier, above note 6.

9. D. B. Harden, *The Phoenicians,* 2d ed. (Harmondsworth, 1971).

10. This corrects my premature attempt to lower substantially the date for the earliest use of the Tophet (H. Hurst and L. E. Stager, "A Metropolitan Landscape: The Late Punic Port of Carthage," *World Archaeology* 9 [1978]: 334–46). That opinion was based on Tanit II-type urns that were found in pits cut into bedrock in areas 2–3. These urns correspond to phases V through VI and indicate a later expansion of the Tophet to the east of area 1 where early groups of burials were discovered in the 1978 season.

11. C. Schaeffer, 1956. Oral communication reported in *CRAI,* 1956, p. 67.

12. M. Weinfeld, "The Worship of Molech and of the Queen of Heaven and Its Background," *Ugarit-Forschungen* 4 (1972): 133–54.

13. Diodorus 20. 14. 4–7. Trans. R. M. Geer, Loeb Classical Library (Cambridge, Mass., 1962).

14. J. H. Schwartz, "The Sacrificed Remains from the Tophet, Carthage," in *Carthage Excavations, 1976–77: Punic Project, Second Interim Report*, ed. L. E. Stager (Chicago, in press).

15. *Scholia* to Plato's *Republic*, 337A.

16. See P. G. Mosca, J. H. Schwartz, and L. E. Stager, above note 7.

17. See Mosca, "Child Sacrifice," above note 7.

18. J. Richard, *Etude médico-légale des urnes sacrificielles puniques et leur contenu* (M.D. diss., Institut Médico-Légal de Lille, 1961).

19. E. S. Morgan, *American Slavery, American Freedom: The Ordeal of Colonial Virginia* (New York, 1975).

20. *CIS*, vol. 1, 123.

21. *CIS*, vol. 1, 307.

22. See Mosca, "Child Sacrifice," pp. 55–77 (above note 7). For primary publications see J. and P. Alquier, "Stèles votives à Saturne découvertes près de N'gaous (Algérie)," *CRAI*, 1931, pp. 21–26. J. Carcopino, "Survivances par substitution des sacrifices d'enfants dans l'Afrique romaine," *Revue de l'histoire des religions* 106 (1932): 592–99. R. Charlier, "La nouvelle série de stèles puniques de Constantine et la question des sacrifices dits 'Molchomor' en relation avec l'expression *BSRM BTM*," *Karthago* 4 (1953): 1–48.

23. H. Hurst and L. E. Stager, "A Metropolitan Landscape."

II. Town Planning and Domestic Architecture of the Early Second Century B.C. on the Byrsa, Carthage

Serge Lancel, Gérard Robine, Jean-Paul Thuillier

The discovery of several houses or elements of houses on the south slopes of Byrsa hill in the 1950s was a turning point in the history of Punic archaeology in Carthage (fig. 2–1). Previously, some remains of domestic architecture of the Punic period had been exposed at various points of the site but in a very sporadic way, and they were not of any significant extent.[1] However, the importance of the discovery was somewhat fogged by the diggers themselves, Père J. Ferron and M. Pinard, who, on the one hand, failed to give a thorough publication of the remains, and, on the other hand, assumed that these houses were of the Gracchan period owing to some coincidence they noticed between the orientation of the walls and the orientation of the rural centuriation of Roman Carthage, which is reputed to be of Gracchan origin.[2] But, as G. Charles-Picard pointed out as early as 1958,[3] not only the building materials (walls, pavements, stuccos) but also the many pieces of equipment found out at floor level in these houses (and accurately published by the excavators:[4] mostly pottery, coins, and Rhodian amphoras stamps) clearly pointed to the late Punic period, between the second half of the third century B.C. and the beginning of the second. We will turn back afterward both to the question of orientation and to the matter of the date, which unexpectedly appeared to be later than previously stated.

At this upper Punic level, going on in the dig in the area first uncovered by P. Ferron, our purpose was mainly to enlarge the excavated area to a more significant extent. In spite of great difficulties due to the depth of Augustan fill above the rubble of the 146 B.C. destruction,[5] we may now report on a coherent quarter including several blocks that appear to be a product of intentional town planning. These blocks or *insulae*—if one may speak Latin dealing with Punic remains—that are partly or entirely known (in the case of two of them) are divided by streets meeting at right angles. We have already three certain streets, and a probable fourth, and at least one crossroad or little square (fig. 2-2). These streets show the average range of width of the Hellenistic period,[6] that is between 6 and 7 meters, with some slight variations from one to another and with no great accuracy in the layout itself. Street I is about 6.50 meters wide, while street II is 7 meters[7] and street III 5.60 meters, widening up to 6 meters toward the northeast. They are very plain roads of packed earth, with some sand refill from time to time, when the roadway became too littered with broken pots and all sorts of domestic rubbish. It seems very likely that the *koprologoi*, the garbage collectors of classical Athens, did not have parallels in Hellenistic Carthage, so plentiful are our finds of pottery and bones in these street layers.[8] In fact, street structures appear to have been reduced to a minimum: sewers are simply dug in the axis of the roadway, and are frequently lined with amphora bodies fitted together; the waste waters running along the corridors of each house were carried into the middle of the street in the same way.[9]

At the intersection of streets II and III, three steps on each roadway (fig. 2-3), converging at right angles at the south corner of block C, made up for the gradient, which is about 16 to 17 percent, especially on street II running northwest to southeast.[10] With these steps, cart traffic was not possible, only pedestrian and probably also donkey traffic. The partial clearing of this square and the stratigraphic study of the accumulation over the steps indicated that these steps, abutting against the waterproof coating of the outside walls of the blocks, were subsequent to that coating. The addition of these steps therefore marks the last phase in the urbanistic development of the quarter, very likely a few years before the destruction of the city in 146 B.C.

With regard to the layout of the blocks, we are now able to make a first approach to the allotments of two blocks that are completely known, B and C.

Block C is 31.30 meters long and 15.65 meters wide, an exact ratio of one to two—something that could not have happened by mere chance. These measures, if expressed in the great Punic cubit of 52.18 centimeters, are respectively sixty cubits for the length and thirty cubits for the width, as our architect noticed on his restored plan (fig. 2-4).[11] These round figures are likely to be highly significant, since the Punic architect very probably used for his urbanistic planning a sexagesimal scale of Babylonian origin.[12] We know, of course, that another standard, a smaller cubit of about 44 centimeters, was also in use, but seemingly not for town planning or house measurement.

This ratio of one to two, expressed in a sixty cubit basis, seems to have been intended also in block A and block E, which, for a still unknown length, show the same measure of thirty cubits in their lesser dimension.

But if we consider block B, which has been entirely uncovered like block C, we get evidence that a smaller type of block has also been planned for this quarter, with the same width of thirty cubits (15.65 m), but with a measure of 10.50 meters in front (a little more than twenty cubits). Unfortunately, it is now impossible to check whether block D, opposite on the other side of street III, had the same measures.

It is in any case quite certain that block B was divided into two house-units, each measuring a little more than ten cubits in width from wall center to wall center. Therefore, a more or less precise ratio of one to three had been intended in the case of these two houses.

Thus we have to consider whether the primary module in the planning of the whole quarter was the block (of which there are two types, the second being a submultiple of the first) or the house, for the house-unit module with the same ratio one to three occurs as well in block C. But in this block the first unit in the southwest end appears to be double, and in fact, instead of six houses, there are in this block only five houses, out of which four are simple house-units.

Before passing to the internal division of the block, it is worth emphasizing the originality of this choice, which seems, as far as we know, to be without precedent in comparable sites.

Of course, among the many ancient urban sites showing orthogonal layout, several examples are already known of town planning in which the planning did not begin with a network of streets to be more or less freely filled in later, but where the basic module of the city grid was the block or *insula*, with standardized dimensions, and a more or less systematically organized interior. The first of these examples is Olynthus, where, as early as the second half of the fifth century, the blueprint of the new city appears to have been laid out on the basis of blocks measuring 300 feet by 120 feet:[13] in Byrsa we are very far from these dimensions. In Olynthus, more freedom can be noticed in the internal development of the blocks, which are divided by alleys (*ambitus*) on the longitudinal axis.

A little later, about the middle of the fourth century B.C., the grid of the new city of Priene provides a rather satisfactory parallel, with small blocks of 160 feet by 120 feet (47.20 m for the length and 35.40 m for the width).[14] The choice of this smaller block module is probably to be explained, as in Byrsa, by field conditions and by the steep gradient of the slope. But here the comparison comes to a stop, since in Priene, as in Sicilian Solunto, the *stenopoi* running downhill are really narrow *angiportus* with continuous steps.

Solunto is likely the closest parallel to our late Punic Byrsa, even if the foundation of the new Sicilian city is to be placed about two centuries earlier, in the very beginning of the fourth century B.C.[15] In Solunto as in Byrsa the interior of the *insula* appears to have been systematically organized into six standard house-units. But, in the same way as in Olynthus, blocks are divided lengthwise by narrow *ambitus*, and, moreover, the dimensions of the basic module (80 m by 40 m, showing also a ratio of two to one) greatly exceed those of Byrsa's blocks.

To summarize this short discussion, we probably have to give an affirmative answer to the question recently put by B. S. J. Isserlin—whether, in the case of intentional planning, the basic conception is not of Hippodamian-Greek rather than Phoenician-Carthaginian origin for Punic cities.[16] That is clear for Punic Selinus in Sicily,[17] as well as for Evesperides in Cyrenaica.[18] In the case of Byrsa at the end of the Hellenistic period, a strong Greek influence is hardly surprising; but in this special case there was probably more Phoenician-Carthaginian than Greek influence in the shape of the small and thickset blocks, as high as they were wide, described in Appian's account of six-storied buildings between the agora and the Byrsa.[19] But, as we shall see elsewhere, precisely this question of stories is a moot point.

With regard to the internal division of the blocks, significant progress has been made since the time when G. Charles-Picard, relying on the results of the excavations of the 1950s, could write: "There was no question here of a central courtyard to give light and air. These both came exclusively from the street. The rooms were square or rectangular, and were juxtaposed without any thought for architectural effect."[20] The comparison with Kerkouane's larger houses, with a central court, sometimes with a peristyle, was hard on Byrsa's tiny and shabby habitations. But we know now that early second century Byrsa did not remain on the fringe of the great architectural development of the Hellenistic period.

For example, in the northeast end of block C, house number 4 appears to be a typical house, laid out around a little courtyard (fig.

2–5).[21] The only access from the street is by way of a narrow corridor 5.50 meters long, 0.90 meter wide, leading to the courtyard.[22] This corridor was probably closed by a door on the street (the threshold and even the outside wall of the building have disappeared here under huge Roman foundations); it was certainly closed at the entrance to the courtyard by a wooden *claustra*, the sill for which still remains. Thus the privacy of the house was well preserved, especially for those who were living and working in the courtyard. The pavement is, for the court as well as for the corridor, a *terrazzo-signinum* or cement-type pavement with many inclusions of yellowish and greenish terra-cotta fragments, and a more or less regular setting of white marble *tessellae*.

The rooms at street level open on the courtyard. It may be that in a first period there were only two rooms at street level, a portico supported by two rectangular pillars giving some extension to the open court on the northwest side. In this phase, the northwest room, beyond the portico, with simple beaten earth floor, was a service room. In a second phase, two thin walls of mud bricks just laid down on the cement floor of the portico divided it into three very small rooms, one of which is clearly a small bathroom: its *opus tessellatum*-type floor made with terra-cotta *tessellae* lies directly on the previous cement floor.[23] The two other rooms, which are very small and narrow, may have been *cellae cubiculariae*. The room toward the southeast (room 1), on street III, probably remained unchanged. A threshold shows that the room opened through a door on the courtyard, and a recess found in one of the walls could be interpreted as a *lararium* or more plainly as a lamp recess.[24] In spite of its good situation, this room can hardly have been an *oecus maior*, owing to its very modest dimensions (only 4.50 m by 3.20 m). It seems in fact that street-level rooms must have been mostly service rooms. That is quite sure for the domestic room at the north angle of block D; the very low ceiling (no more than 1.80 m high), and the discovery of a rotary mill, with *catillus* and *meta* in situ, leave no doubt that the chamber served as a millroom.[25]

If, as previously proposed, the house-unit module is in fact this narrow house of roughly 15 meters by 5 meters, probably two cases of double house-units (15 m by 10 m) are recognizable, one at the southwest end of block C, the other in the southwest part of block E. In the case of these double house-units, the layout is of course different. For example, in the double house of Block E, partly excavated in July 1978, the entrance is not on the main axis, it is a side entrance, on street II (but it seems that a main entrance from street III, leading directly to the courtyard, is to be restored). From street II, this side entrance gave access to a little lobby, part of which was separated by a thin dividing wall of stuccoed mud bricks so as to form a small bathroom or *lavatrina* (we did not find any bath structure or bathtub) with a water conduit in the angle. The floor, as in the case of another bathroom noted above,[26] is a mosaic of terra-cotta *tessellae;* a wooden *claustra* separated this shower cabin or *lavatrina* from the lobby, and the waste water was carried into the street by way of a shallow gutter passing through the lobby below the *claustra* and the threshold. This double house is only partly cleared, but in the present state of the excavation we may already recognize a small central court-yard, measuring 2.50 meters by 2.50 meters, bordered by a portico on three sides. The pavement of the courtyard is of *terrazzo-signinum* type with a regular setting of white marble *tessellae.* In the middle of the courtyard is the *impluvium* collecting rain water and also set in the pave-ment is the outlet of the overflow pipe of the cistern which underlies the courtyard (fig. 2–6). A beautiful threshold of gray-blue limestone, 1.80 meters wide, gives access to a room with carefully stuccoed walls and fine *terrazzo-signinum*-type pavement. This room, measuring 5 meters by 3.40 meters, we shall venture to call an *oecus maior* with more assurance than we felt in the previous case of house number 4 of block C.

With the exception of double units, the houses of Byrsa were small: only 75 square meters, out of which a certain part was open to the sky (corridors, courtyards). We must, however, assume the existence of two or three stories, perhaps more, above the street level. This assumption is supported by some data given by the excavation. First, the outside walls in all the buildings are strong and thick and are made with large, dressed blocks of El Haouaria sandstone; they were thus able to bear high and heavy superstructures. Besides, the number and capacity of the cisterns show that they were not provided only for the few occupants at ground level; thus there are four large bathtub-shaped cisterns for the two house-units of block B;[27] block C includes eight cisterns (each single house-unit has a large and deep bathtub-shaped cistern—and even two in the case of house number 5—and the double house at the southwest end of the block has three cisterns, two of which are deep bottle-shaped cisterns).[28] Moreover, we found a great amount of fragmentary flooring in the upper levels of the destruction debris inside the houses; this is also a good hint that there was at least a second floor, and probably more. In one place we can notice on the coping of an outside wall—but toward the inside of the house—the traces of a *terrazzo-signinum*-type second floor.

So it is very tempting to recognize in these buildings of Byrsa's south slope, along this street II, which is in fact running down toward the harbors, these famous "houses built closely together and six storeys high," which were "along three streets ascending from the Forum to the fortress" of Byrsa.[29] Appian goes on to say that when, during the battle, the Romans had become masters of the first few houses of the quarter, "they put timbers across over the narrow passage-ways, and crossed as on bridges." Now, we have seen that, even though they are not really narrow *stenopoi*, streets III and I, which would have to be crossed over by Roman soldiers going toward the top of the hill, are respectively 5.60 meters and 6.50 meters wide, and could have been crossed in the way related by Appian. So, our archaeological data are not inconsistent with Appian's account and description. The only unsolved problem is that, at least so far, we have not found the slightest evidence for staircases inside the houses. But built staircases would hardly have found room enough in these narrow houses, and they may well have been wooden staircases, as often in Olynthus and Delos.[30] Moreover, we have good indication that in some places (along the small side of block A and, in street I, along the northwest side of block C) access to the upper floors was provided by outside staircases encroaching upon the roadway.

We hope forthcoming excavations will give more satisfactory answers to the problem of the height of the buildings. Meanwhile a few words more are needed on some technical details of construction. The materials with which the walls were built are very diverse, showing several sorts of jointing. The thin dividing walls inside each house are mostly of mudbrick masonry, often standing on small-stone masonry for the foot of the wall. A very common material for partition walls between the houses is the *opus mixtum* or *opus Africanum,* with strong and thick braces of big ashlars strengthening masonry of small stones. As we have previously seen, main walls—that is, outside walls—were strongly built with large, dressed blocks of sandstone, showing the thickness of the large Punic cubit (0.52 m); but they often appear to be reused blocks, with preexisting stucco coating. Especially worth noting is a remarkable feature of the outside face of the walls limiting the blocks on the streets, and still noticeable at several points on blocks C and E: a thick and tall packing of rubble, sometimes up to 1.5 meters high, carefully lined with a waterproof coating, that covers as well the upper part of the wall (fig. 2–7). This coating was remade from time to time, and, on the small side of block C on street IV the last remaking is clearly contemporaneous with the last rubbish layers of the roadway. As far as we know only one certain parallel can be cited for this feature, namely in the American excavations of Morgantina in Sicily, in structures dating probably to the end of the third century B.C.[31] Such a feature was seemingly a protection against the undermining action of rainwater in streets of steep declivity, which lacked, as we have seen before, an adequate system of draining. With this thick and tall reinforcement all around them, these Punic *insulae* were really like small islands emerging from streets that heavy winter rains changed into torrents.

In Morgantina the reinforcement of the walls is to be dated toward the end of the third century B.C. What about the date of our Punic blocks in Byrsa? In all the destruction layers close above the floors, but mainly in all soundings made under the floors or under sealed levels we have collected plain black-glaze pottery from central Italy, the so-called Campanian A.[32] Since there is little chance—as J.-P. Morel, especially, thinks—that this type of pottery coming from Ischia and Naples might have reached African shores before the first years of the second century B.C., we have here a *terminus post quem* that puts this urbanistic development, at the earliest, after the end of the Second Punic War. Probably we may be more precise, thanks to many Rhodian amphora stamps found in the destruction layers near the floors,[33] like the stamp bearing the name of Nysios, a Rhodian merchant whose activity has been dated about 180 B.C. by Virginia Grace.[34] In the foundation trench of block B, at the south angle of the block, we found a Rhodian stamp which gives the name of Pratophanes, a priest of Helios whose priesthood is to be dated probably a few years before 180 B.C.[35] Thus we are now able to be more specific, lowering appreciably the dates previously proposed.[36] Block B, and therefore all these blocks, which were evidently planned in one piece and built at the same time or in close succession as a product of intentional town planning, appear to be very late. The construction of block B may be put toward the end of the first quarter of the second century B.C.; perhaps a slightly earlier date may be proposed for block C, which underwent more changes through the insertion of dividing walls and the remaking of pavements.[37] It seems quite clear now that people lived in these houses during less than half a century, between the years following Hannibal's last magistracy in 196 B.C., and the destruction of the city in 146.

The most important fact to emerge is that this quarter of late Punic Carthage is a new quarter, without previous history as a residential district. About the middle of the seventh century B.C. the south slope of Byrsa began to be used as a cemetery, with graves datable down to the beginning of the sixth century, running down perhaps to the end of the sixth century on the lower slope and westward on the same slope.[38] Then the field lay unused for three centuries until iron workers established workshops that seem to have been active between the middle of the third century and the very first years of the second.[39] So these blocks and their habitations are products of peace restored after the Second Punic War, and they can be regarded as a palpable effect of this revival and of the renewed prosperity that Appian reports.[40] Furthermore, this late urbanistic development in a vacant area that was also such an important and valuable place, on this slope facing the sea and the harbors, may very probably represent a state initiative, carried out in a technocratic manner, with the layout of standard houses, small but well finished, and seemingly intended to be occupied by a homogeneous group of people (perhaps priests or officers?).

This recognition of Byrsa's late Punic district compels us to face up again to the persistent problem of Hellenistic Carthage. The literary evidence dealing with the internal topography of the city is relatively rich, as we know, for the time of the Punic Wars, but it is wanting for earlier periods. However, too little attention has been paid to Diodorus Siculus' description. The passage is rightly quoted by H. Hurst and L. Stager, but, in our opinion, not correctly interpreted by them.[41] Diodorus tells us that Bomilcar, attempting a coup d'état in the years of Agathocles's expedition 308 B.C., reviewed his forces, mercenaries, and citizens in a district called New City, a short distance from Old Carthage.[42] Then they moved from this *Nea Polis* to the agora, killing everyone in the streets who resisted.[43] But the Carthaginians recovered and, after occupying the tall buildings surrounding the agora, showered missiles on the rebels and compelled them "to force their way back by narrow streets to the New City, being continuously struck with missiles from the houses they passed by." Finally, Bomilcar and his supporters stopped and occupied a position on a hill.[44] This text is clear: Bomilcar moves from the New City to the Old City, toward the agora, which we know from Appian's account to have been situated near the harbors;[45] when he is obliged to retire, he has then, turning back to *Nea Polis,* to walk up by *stenopoi* (narrow streets) and between houses, toward a hill *(hyperdexios tis topos).* This hill is not called Byrsa, and could not be Byrsa, not at least the south slope of our Byrsa, since we know that at this time, at the end of the fourth century B.C., there were not yet houses in the place. This disturbs the striking parallel between the ascending movement of Scipio's soldiers going from the agora to Byrsa in 146 and the ascending movement of Bomilcar and his companions in 308 B.C. But it is also clear that we can no longer agree with H. Hurst and L. Stager who inferred from Diodorus' text that "the late Punic port and the grid pattern buildings might all be part of New Carthage, the Old City perhaps lying towards the north."[46] According to Diodorus' description, indeed, the *Nea Polis* is clearly somewhere on the curved line of hills between Byrsa's east slope and Bordj Djedid, and perhaps even beyond this line, as believed by St. Gsell.[47] The location of the Old City remains a moot question, but it remains probable that it stretched in the little coastal plain along the shore, northward up to Bordj Djedid's first slopes and southward down to the Tophet district. On the one hand, new houses and new quarters are very frequently built in an Old City (and we think of the late Punic houses exposed by the German team along the shore halfway between the harbors and Bordj Djedid) and, on the other hand, we cannot agree with the recent statement according to which the Tophet would not have been in use earlier than the fourth century B.C.[48] We persist in thinking that the first deposits in the Tophet are to be dated to the end of the eighth century, and we continue to believe with D. Harden that "it is highly improbable that such a precinct... would have lain outside the settlement area."[49]

   Is it now possible to be more precise regarding the urban expansion of Hellenistic Carthage on the basis of the archaeological data at our disposal? We will not deal here with the problem of harbors, though it is now clear, thanks to the Hurst and Stager teams, that the harbors play an important role in this great question.[50] Moreover, as a preliminary re- mark, we would like to point out that in many areas where urbanization gained ground in Carthage during the Hellenistic period the houses were probably not very dense, at least in this *Nea Polis* (perhaps a part of the little later so-called *Megara*) where Bomilcar could review some 4,500 soldiers.[51] Secondly, we must always bear in mind that the separation between the living and the dead was not necessarily as strict in Carthage as it was in classical Greece, where we know some significant excep- tions.[52] Large areas, like Odeon's plateau, Bordj Djedid, and Sainte- Monique hill (now Saida) continued to be from the fourth century on- ward like enclaves, always used for funeral purposes, in the growing urban tissue of the Hellenistic city.[53] Since the limits between the living and the dead were not clear-cut, owing also to the hilly and undulating terrain, we cannot expect that the new quarters were built according to a uniform grid. It has been stated, both by C. Picard and P. Cintas, that at the time of the Punic Wars several districts of Carthage had been built with a single orientation, southwest to northeast.[54] That seems to be right for the coastal plain, and, so far as these excavations have been correctly reported, it appears that several elements of houses, loosely dated between the fourth and the second centuries, show roughly the same orientation parallel to the coastline, well attested now by the German discoveries along the shore as used since the beginning of the third century.[55] But only by mere chance three late Punic cisterns exposed by Ch. Saumagne on the south slope of Juno hill appear to be roughly in coincidence with the Julian cadastration, which also follows the coastline.[56] On Byrsa hill, which is now the best known area for late Punic urbanization, we can see that, turning round the hill from the east to the southwest slope, the buildings follow the contours in a very flexible manner. In *Byrsa I* will shortly be presented a previously unpublished report by Ch. Saumagne on excavations made in 1925 on some Punic levels of Byrsa's east slope.[57] This report shows two groups of walls and cisterns, the first of which, toward the north near the Roman *cardo* IV east, is seven to eight degrees north-northeast, while the second, at one angle of the Roman *decumanus maximus* and *cardo* V east, is twenty-three to twenty-four degrees northeast, that is to say diverging just a little westward from the direction of the *cardo*. These two groups of Punic remains are very likely to be dated roughly in the third century, owing to the techniques of the pavements that are made of large hexagonal and diamond-shaped terra-cotta tiles. Lower down on the same slope, toward the southeast, a recent rescue excavation directed by F. Chalbi has uncovered a Punic house probably dating from the beginning of the third century, with an orientation diverging by twenty degrees eastward from that of the subsequent Roman *cardo* VII east.

Toward the west, the orientation changes appreciably: our blocks diverge by thirty-five to thirty-six degrees eastward from the Roman grid, and elements of another group west of these blocks are almost exactly east to west, diverging by twenty-one to twenty-two degrees from the orientation of the blocks.[58] Of all these individually planned sectors radiating on the slopes of Byrsa hill, the houses of the area under current French excavation seem to be the latest. Now that their date is established, they remind us of a famous phrase, for they have been left to us as the most tangible part of Hannibal's legacy.

NOTES

The text of this paper has been kindly revised by Professor Homer A. Thompson of the Institute for Advanced Study at Princeton to whom we are greatly indebted for various corrections and suggestions.

1. See note 55 below.
2. Cf. *Cahiers de Byrsa* 5 (1955): 80–81.
3. G. Picard, "Un quartier de maisons puniques à Carthage," *RA* 1 (1958): 21–32. See also, C. Picard, "Vestiges d'un édifice punique à Carthage," *Karthago* 3 (1951): 124.
4. Cf. *Cahiers de Byrsa* 5 (1955): 61–68, and 9 (1960–61): 99–114, on Rhodian amphora stamps.
5. In some places, we now have banks more than 7 m high.
6. Cf. R. Martin, *L'urbanisme dans la Grèce antique,* 2d ed. (Paris, 1974), p. 207.
7. It is worth pointing out that this wider street—not wide enough, however, to be rightly called a *plateia*—runs toward the southeast toward the harbors.
8. Cf. Cl. Vatin, "Jardins et services de voirie," *BCH* 100 (1975): 555–64.
9. The statement according to which "ces rues étaient pourvues d'égouts bâtis comme ceux des villes grecques de Sicile" [G. and C. Charles-Picard, *La vie quotidienne à Carthage* (Paris, 1958), p. 47; cf. also G. Charles-Picard, *Life and Death of Carthage* (London, 1968), p. 283] is based on a misconception dating from a time before the excavation was sufficiently advanced: cf. C. Picard, in *Karthago* 3 (1951): 124 and fig. 1, p. 120.
10. See also S. Lancel, in *CRAI,* 1978, pp. 311–15.
11. For Punic metrology see, most recently, B. S. J. Isserlin and Joan du Plat Taylor, *Motya* (Leiden, 1974), 1: 93–95, who tried for the site of Motya to identify measurements either in Attic feet or in royal or great cubits of 52.5 cm–or a little less. It seems that both systems of measurement were in use in Hellenistic Motya in Sicily.
12. For example, the temple built by King Solomon "was sixty cubits long by twenty cubits broad, and its height was thirty cubits" (I *Kings* 6:2). For the sexagesimal scale, see O. Neugebauer, *The Exact Sciences in Antiquity* (Princeton, 1952) chap. 6; and idem, *A History of Ancient Mathematical Astronomy,* (Berlin, 1975), especially pt. 3, bk. 6, "Mathematical Concepts," pp. 1113–32.
13. Cf. D. M. Robinson and J. Walter Graham, *Excavations at Olynthus* (Baltimore, 1938), vol. 8, *The Hellenic House,* pp. 29–51; cf. also A. Giuliano, *Urbanistica delle città greche* (Milano, 1966), pp. 88–91; R. Martin, *L'urbanisme dans la Grèce antique,* 2d ed. (Paris, 1974), pp. 110–11.
14. Cf. Th. Wiegand and H. Schrader, *Priene* (Berlin, 1904), pp. 48–56, 68–80, and 285–300; A. Giuliano, *Urbanistica delle città greche,* pp. 122–26; R. Martin, *L'urbanisme dans la Grèce antique,* pp. 113–15.
15. For Solunto see especially L. Natoli di Cristina, "Caratteri della cultura abitativa Solutina," in *Scritti in onore di Salvatore Caronia* (Palermo, 1965) pp. 175–98.
16. Cf. B. S. J. Isserlin, "Some Common Features in Phoenician/Punic Town-Planning," *Rivisita di studi Fenici* 1 (1973): 135–54, especially p. 137.

17. Cf. A. di Vita, "L'elemento Punico a Selinunte nel IV e nel III Sec. A. C.," *Archeologia classica* 5 (1953): 39–47; R. Martin, *Kokalos* 21 (1975): 54–67 and *CRAI*, 1977, pp. 46–63.

18. Cf. Isserlin, "Phoencian/Punic Town-Planning," p. 150, fig. 6.

19. Appian *Libyca* 128.

20. Cf. C. and G..Charles-Picard, *La vie quotidienne à Carthage* (Paris, 1958), p. 47; most recently, G. Charles-Picard, *Life and Death of Carthage*, p. 283. The same statement in D. B. Harden, *The Phoenicians*, 1st ed. (New York, 1962), p. 136: "The plans are simple with groups of rectangular rooms without architectural pretensions."

21. See a description of this house by J.-P. Thuillier in *Byrsa I: rapports préliminaires des fouilles (1974–1976)*, ed. S. Lancel et al. Collection de l'ecole française de Rome no. 41 (Rome, 1979), pp. 228–32.

22. Another access from street I at higher level is perhaps possible (cf. fig. 2–5) and an independent access to room I from street III may be hypothetically restored.

23. These *opus tessellatum*-type pavements made with terra-cotta *tessellae* are among the commonest features of late Punic floors in Carthage; these *tessellae*, roughly 2.5 cm square with a thickness of about 1 cm, must have been obtained by cutting up the walls of large vessels, as it is shown by the sides, one slightly convex, one slightly concave, this latter bearing clear traces of turning on the wheel. But the edges of the *tessellae* show that they were cut before the firing of the vessel. The turning of a large cylinder (probably about 50 cm in diameter) was the only practical way to obtain almost flat *tessellae* of small dimensions.

24. It has quite completely disappeared now, but cf. *Cahiers de Byrsa* 9 (1960–61): 97.

25. The closest parallel for this rotary mill is to be found in D. White, "A Survey of Millstones from Morgantina," *AJA* 67 (1963): 199–206, especially pp. 202–3, type 3 (pl. 47, figs. 6 and 7), dated at the end of the third century B.C. (p. 205).

26. See p. 17 and note 23 above.

27. The average range of depth of these bathtub-shaped cisterns is between 3.5 m and 4 m.

28. One of these bottle-shaped cisterns is 6.10 m deep and 2 m to 2.50 m in diameter (cf. *Byrsa* I [1979], p. 77).

29. Appian *Libyca* 128. Trans. H. White, Loeb Classical Library (Cambridge, Mass., 1958).

30. For Olynthus, cf. D. M. Robinson and J. W. Graham, *Excavations at Olynthus* 8: 267–80; for Delos, cf. J. Chamonard, *Delos* (Paris, 1923–24), 8: 305–18; lastly, Ph. Bruneau, "Deliaca," *BCH* 99 (1975): 274, who assumes that in certain cases movable ladders could have been in use.

31. Cf. R. Stillwell, "Excavations at Sierra Orlando 1958, Preliminary Report III," *AJA* 63 (1959): 167, and pl. 40, fig. 4.

32. In other words, the type I of Doris Taylor at Cosa.

33. These are to be added to the many items collected in the excavations of the 1950s by J. Ferron and M. Pinard (cf. p. 14 and note 4).

34. Cf. *Delos*, 27: 304–5: *Nysios* appear to be connected with the eponym *Pausanias* of period IV, 180–146 B.C.

35. Cf. *CRAI*, 1978, p. 310, and V. Grace, in *Delos*, 27: 294 and 301.

36. Cf. *CRAI*, 1976, pp. 65–66, 76–77, and also *AntAfr* 11 (1977): 47–48.

37. Some of these changes, which resulted in very small *cellae cubiculariae* inside the houses, could perhaps be explained by the necessity of receiving refugees expelled by the continual encroachment of Numidians on the inland Punic area during this period.

38. For graves of seventh century below the houses, cf. S. Lancel, in *CRAI*, 1978, pp. 323–27; for previous excavations of cemeteries of the sixth century, by P. Delattre, P. Lapeyre, and Ch. Saumagne, cf. *Byrsa I* (1979), pp. 17–27 and 28–31.

39. Cf. *CRAI*, 1978, pp. 317–23. Some hints of this type of activity were given by Ch. Saumagne's excavations of the foot of the south slope: cf. *Byrsa I* (1979), pp. 29–30.

40. Appian *Libyca* 67: "... fifty years, during which Carthage, blessed with unbroken peace, advanced greatly in population and power by reason of the fertility of her soil and her advantageous position on the coast."

41. H. Hurst and L. Stager, "A Metropolitan Landscape: The Late Punic Port of Carthage," *World Archaeology* 9, no. 3, (1978): pp. 340–41; but see also St. Gsell, *HAAN*, vol. 2, pp. 14–15.

42. Diod. 20. 44. 1.

43. Diod. 20. 44. 2–3.

44. Diod. 20. 44. 4–5.

45. Appian *Libyca* 127.

46. H. Hurst and L. Stager, "Metropolitan Landscape," p. 341.

47. St. Gsell, *HAAN*, vol. 2, p. 15 and n. 1, where Gsell assumed that *Nea Polis* might have been at Sidi bou Said or near Djebel el-Khaoui, which seems too distant to agree with Diodorus's statement.

48. H. Hurst and L. Stager, "Metropolitan Landscape," p. 338. This view is seemingly accepted by J. Humphrey in "North African News Letter I," *AJA* 82 (1978): 514.

49. D. B. Harden, *The Phoenicians*, 1st ed., p. 34 (2d ed., 1971, p. 31). This is not the place to discuss the chronology of the Tophet. Let us say simply: (1) that the chronology of early Punic pottery proposed by D. Harden (*AJA* 41 [1927]: 297–310 and *Iraq* 4 [1937]: 59–89) and P. Cintas (*Céramique punique* [Paris, 1950], pp. 490–517, and *Manuel d'archéologie punique* (Paris, 1970), 1: 324–75) cannot be easily lowered by some three centuries; (2) that evidently there is not a single area in the precinct of Tanit at Salammbô, but at least two and probably more areas in which the dating of the deepest levels cannot be uniform.

50. Since it seems that the structures corresponding with Appian's description (*Libyca* 96) are not to be dated prior to the late fourth century B.C. (H. Hurst, "Excavations at Carthage 1975: Second Interim Report," *AntJ* 56 (1975): 177–97; H. Hurst and L. Stager, "Metropolitan Landscape," pp. 341–44).

51. Diod. 20. 44. 1.

52. At least in Hellenistic times in Carthage cemeteries existed within the city *(intra muros):* cf. St. Gsell, *HAAN*, vol. 2, pp. 13, 19; also D. B. Harden, "The Topography of Punic Carthage," *Greece and Rome,* 9, no. 25 (1939): 5: "there is no evidence that burial was forbidden within the area of Phoenician towns." This is, of course, of great importance topographically, since the argument from the location of the cemeteries is not cogent for the delimitation of the city. For infractions of the rule in sixth-century Athens, see R. S. Young, "Sepulturae intra urbem," *Hesperia* 20 (1951): 67–134. A similar example in Tarentum is referred to by St. Gsell, *HAAN,* vol. 2, p. 19.

53. Cf. P. Cintas, *Manuel d'archéologie punique* (Paris, 1976), 2: 239–387; and lastly H. Benichou-Safar, "Carte des nécropoles puniques de Carthage," *Karthago* 27 (1976): 5–35.

54. Cf. C. Picard, *Karthago* 3 (1951): 126 and P. Cintas, *Manuel,* 2: 124–25 and fig. 9.

55. In the district called Dermech, in the northwest part of the little coastal plain: "Maison du Paon" (Ch. Saumagne, *BAC*, 1934–35, pp. 51–58), "maison du terrain Clariond" (M. Vézat, *BAC,* 1946–49, pp. 676–78), "maison du terrain des héritiers Grosjean" (P. Cintas, *Manuel,* 1: 441, cf. also *Manuel,* 2: map 4, point 37); also near the Carthage railroad station (P. Cintas, *Manuel,* 1: 441, 2: 125 and map 4, point 36).

56. Cf. Ch. Saumagne, *BAC,* 1930–31, 641–59.

57. The first part of the report dealing with the Roman remains uncovered in this area has been published already: Ch. Saumagne, in *BAC,* 1924, pp. 177–93. For Punic remains, see *Byrsa I* (1979), 300–1.

58. Cf. S. Lancel, *CRAI,* 1978, pp. 327–29.

III. The Plan of Roman Carthage: Practicalities and Politics

Edith Mary Wightman

To all students of Carthage, or indeed of Roman urban planning, the city's regular long narrow *insulae* stretching parallel to the sea form a familiar pattern. A coherent picture of their dimensions and those of the overall grid that they comprise was first worked out by Saumagne, whose figures were subsequently refined in certain points of practical detail by Davin.[1] Recent excavations have in general confirmed these scholars' views, and it now causes no surprise when excavation at a point indicated by surveyors' calculations uncovers a street or crossroad. Rather, surprise is elicited and a special explanation sought if a contrary result emerges. Nevertheless, there remain a few problems and oddities to which attention may usefully be drawn. These in turn will be found to lead to the consideration of wider questions, and to the need for the coordination of observations made in the field with the framework derived from historical sources.

It must be remembered that the measurements given for streets and *insulae* have been conceived in two different ways. The method employed by Saumagne was to think principally in terms of Roman measurements, although the figures were of course based on actual observed remains of streets. The intended dimensions of the *insulae* thus appeared to be 480 by 120 Roman feet, an observation which has not since been seriously doubted. The twin problems then presented themselves of plotting the lines accurately on a large-scale map and of translating them into precise modern measurements, especially since the Roman foot was susceptible of variations according to place and time: these were not and still have not been totally solved. Davin accepted Saumagne's ideas but concentrated more on the available observed measurements, taking as

starting points the dimensions of major monuments and the distances between the central drains of the known streets. Since individual drains
might not be precisely straight or centered, it was necessary to average a
number of instances. Davin in this way arrived at 42.30 meters for center
to center of the *cardines* and allowed 7 meters (24 Roman ft.) for the
streets, giving a width of 35.30 meters for the *insula* block; he also
reckoned that a short foot of 0.294 meter had been used.[2] These calculations have recently been adopted by the team from the University of
Michigan.[3] The Italian and Canadian surveyors, on the other hand, have
based their calculations on the more normal Roman foot of 0.295 meter,
which gives 42.48 meters for center to center of *cardines*, 7.08 meters
for the streets, and 35.40 meters for the width of the *insulae*.[4] These
differences, while slight in themselves, can give rise to palpable dis-
crepancies when theoretical measurements have to be made over long
distances. Now that a greater number of streets has been uncovered, it is
to be hoped that this tantalizing problem may be capable of resolution.
For while apparently minor and academic, it will be found in the course
of arguments presented below to have a potential bearing on the history
of the site and its surroundings.

A brief comment is also called for on the major axes, traditionally
called *decumanus* and *cardo maximus.* Davin reckoned with a width of
40 Roman feet, since calculations based on the length between central
axes of theater and amphitheater gave 11.50 meters, or between 39 and
40 feet. The French team has recently reported a width of 11.40 meters,
or just under 39 feet, for the *cardo maximus* on the Byrsa.[5] Canadian
calculations have indirectly also indicated that the *cardo maximus* was
indeed wider than the normal streets, though without bringing any
greater precision on this minor point. Again, the views of Saumagne and
Davin appear confirmed.

The second and more speculative part of Saumagne's brilliant observations was his hypothesis on the original planned extent of the city.
This, he argued, theoretically stretched for six *decumani* and twenty *cardines* on either side of the two main axes, *decumanus* and *cardo maximus.*
Confirmation of these original limits is harder to find, since the city
subsequently outgrew them on at least two sides and archaeology uncovers the actual, not the theoretical. Nevertheless certain pertinent observations can be made, including the virtual absence of any irregularities
not explicable in one of three ways: the exigencies of a difficult topography, the need for large public buildings to expand over more than one

of the narrow *insulae,* or developments that were considerably later in date than the original plan, any of which might lead to the suppression of an individual street. In an area that was not built up until the second century A.D., the Italian team found that the street grid had been basically respected.[6] In the area of the second Canadian team *cardo* IV east was missing just south of *decumanus* IV north (figs. 3–1 and 3–4); the building history of this area is however unknown prior to a date that lies probably within the fourth century, and the encroaching building may have been a public one.[7] Similarly, the explanation of other remains shown by the topographical map to encroach on or block streets may be public character or lateness of date.

The only major and puzzling anomalies lie in the Italian sector. First there is the well-laid paving, limiting an *insula* though not necessarily forming a continuous road surface, that extends eastward from the *cardo maximus* below the gate known as Bab el-Riah and has a *terminus post quem* of late second or early third century date. City building at this point did not go beyond it and thus did not extend as far as the theoretical line of *decumanus* VI north. Yet only two and a half *insulae* to the east the second Canadian team has uncovered a partially paved section of *decumanus* VI on its correct line (see figs. 4–2 and 4–3). Belonging to the late fourth or early fifth century, this is clearly the product of a different, later phase of urban development.[8] Questions arising are the original linear extent of the paving to the east—did it in effect form what might be termed a *decumanus Vbis*—and of the later *decumanus* to the west. The first may have to remain unanswered in the foreseeable future, but a possible reason for the creation of a limit here can be suggested, since it is the point at which a major line of the rural centuriation (defining the northeastern side of the square which starts on the La Malga-Byrsa axis) meets the urban *cardo maximus.* The second question may yet be solved by a trench across the bank that continues the line of *decumanus* IV westward to the *cardo maximus* (fig. 3–2).

The paving on the Italian site had later partially served as a foundation for the Theodosian Wall and adjoins the *cardo maximus* just opposite the bank (known generally as the Teurf el-Sour or Boundary Bank) that marks the wall's continuation westward. Building in this sector halted along the line now marked by this bank, which as it proceeds westward increases in height and clarity. This phenomenon is quite distinct from and additional to the missing northwest corner of the otherwise rectangular city plan, where the rural centuriation rather than the urban grid formed the boundary—the latter another point observed by Saumagne, incorporated in his hypothesis, and confirmed by recent excavations. Below the bank, an Italian trench uncovered part of a cemetery.

The obvious conclusion might at first sight seem to be that a natural steep declivity limited expansion. This is however by no means confirmed by results from either the Italian or the adjoining Canadian sector. To take the latter first, a section across the bank where it adjoins an upstanding portion of the Theodosian Wall (fig. 3–3) suggests a totally different origin for the more easterly section of the Teurf el-Sour. The level of the soil today at the top of the bank—that is, inside the line of the wall—is some 5 meters above the present level outside of it, but over 8 meters above the original ground level, which has not in fact been reached. Examination of the strata showed that the bank here was artificial, and that a minimum of 3 meters of fill had been dumped to raise the level of the ground behind the wall at the time that it was built, in or around A.D. 425. The Italian trenches have likewise shown a substantial change in ground level, partly from what might be a natural accumulation of soil, partly from deliberate fill of second and late fourth century date.[9] The bank in this sector, like its continuation in the Canadian, is thus largely or even entirely artificial, its line and height the result of decisions taken to level the ground upward to receive the buildings of a particular period or periods. This was then delimited at certain points by terrace walls (but not along its entire length, since none was found behind the upstanding part of the wall). In the portion examined by the Italian team this terrace wall ran parallel to the street grid, but it cannot have maintained this direction for long. While a natural declivity may well have existed—indeed the lie of the land demands it—both original line and degree of slope are uncertain, and it appears to have been insufficient to call a halt to urbanization. Rather, this was the result of certain deliberated but haphazard actions, taken at a time when the necessity for maintaining and developing the street grid and outer limit or *pomerium* as originally planned (i.e., *decumanus* VI north) was no longer considered to be of vital importance. Once the city was thus delimited in practice, burials of second and fourth century date were laid in territory that lay within the original *pomerium*.

In the northern sector of the town, the physical extent of urbanization is thus shown to be uneven. West of the *cardo maximus* it never reached the theoretical limits represented by *decumanus* VI, and the same seems to be true for at least one *insula* to the east: as seen above, the rural centuriation may have been a determining factor in this last sector. Between *cardines* I and III east it may have reached the limits and respected them; the situation here is not entirely clear at present (fig. 3-2). Between *cardines* III and IX, buildings extended beyond *decumanus* VI for a distance of rather less than the length of an extra *insula:* within this sector, between the lines of *cardines* V and VI, lies the upstanding portion of the Theodosian Wall mentioned above (fig. 3-4). From *cardo* IX eastward, the city's extension northward was considerably greater (fig. 3-5). This last fact is made apparent not only by the line of the wall but also by the existence in the plan of Delattre and Gauckler (recording actual remains rather than giving a theoretical plan) of at least one further *decumanus*. [10] Even in this last area closer to the coast, the regular intervals of the street grid were at least sometimes followed. In the southern part of the city, where a parallel development close to the harbors and shore took place, an additional *decumanus* was found to have the correct orientation but did not lie at the regular interval. [11] The date at which this strip development along the coast occurred (it might be compared with the development of modern Carthage) cannot as yet be dated with precision, but it is clearly analogous to the disregard for the original plan shown in the Italian sector: theory in effect gave way before practical considerations, and the Italian evidence shows that this trend was already present before the end of the second century.

To both north and south, fields (and in the British sector a building) oriented on the rural cadastration seem to have extended right up to the city limits, with the exception of the one bank which continues the line of *decumanus* VI between the Canadian and Italian sectors. [12] North of this, it is possible and even likely that the rural cadastration influenced the building history and eventually the line of the Theodosian Wall. Whether *decumanus* VI ever served as a real rather than a theoretical boundary here is not clear: the Canadian excavations of 1978 suggested that a major building may have straddled it at an early stage of its actual physical development. [13]

The relationship of the rural and urban grids is a question deserving further attention. That the rural centuriation bounded the city on the northwest side seems indisputable, but in view of the evidence presented above for ad hoc developments it might be queried whether this was planned from the period of the foundation. A crucial role in the argument is played by the cisterns at La Malga, which are fitted into the corner of one of the rural centuries. Recently scepticism over the early date sometimes proposed for them has grown, and indeed they make little sense before the building of the aqueduct from Ain Zaghouan, usually placed in the second century.[14] If urbanization had simply not yet reached this area, it might be suggested a rational decision could have been taken in Hadrianic or Antonine times to use the rural grid as the boundary. Although cemeteries have long been known on this side of the city, it was until recently not clear whether burials of the first two centuries are found within the triangular area. In fact, a recent Italian trench on the edge of the triangle (the theoretical crossing of *decumanus* VI and *cardo* VIII west) has uncovered burials of first, second, and third centuries A.D.[15] This provides what had hitherto been lacking, namely substantive evidence that the relevant decision was indeed most likely taken at the inception of the street plan, rather than at some subsequent date. In any case the question leads on to a consideration of both rural and urban grid in their historical context.

A brief summary of what may be termed the received view can readily be given. The rural cadastration belongs either to the years immediately following the conquest in 146 B.C. or to the period of abortive colonization by C. Gracchus in 122 B.C. While the decision to recolonize Carthage was certainly taken by Julius Caesar, and Statilius Taurus, acting as his legate, probably officially settled some colonists in 44 B.C., the real work of recolonization was that of Augustus in the years following Actium. It is to him that are to be attributed the final choice of this site overlying the ancient Punic city and the laying out of the street grid. Both grid systems had however a common point of departure on the Byrsa, a point which now lies just within the apse of the Cathedral of Saint Louis, behind the altar and very nearly on the axis of the building.[16]

The anteriority of the rural cadastration to the urban has remained virtually unquestioned, and indeed there are good arguments to support the view.[17] It is true that the literary sources say nothing of a centuriation following 146 B.C., and leave much to be desired in their account of the activities of C. Gracchus. Unanimity is most nearly achieved in the famous tale that wolves displaced his boundary markers—a tale which was no less effective as propaganda because patently untrue, at least if taken literally.[18] Even so the sources disagree on the nature of the markers, and whether they delimited a city or simply rural divisions.[19] The story does however presuppose some operation of *limitatio*. This is further confirmed by two very different pieces of epigraphical evidence. The first is the inscription, found near La Malga, giving the names of three men who appear to be *III viri* for the assignation of lands active in 121 B.C. after the death of Gracchus. The second is the land law of 111, which regulates the possession of certain lands in Italy, Africa, and near Corinth, and clearly implies that there had been *limitatio* and assignation of lands in Africa, whereas the Corinthian land had apparently still to be measured.[20]

The argument that land measurement may have taken place in the years following the conquest as a symbol of Rome's possession of large areas of *ager publicus* in the new province rests on two bases: the fact that the law of 111 seems to refer to a wider area than the neighborhood of Carthage and the recognition of widespread centuriation on a single orientation covering a large region in the northeast of the province.[21] The early date remains however putative, while it is clear from the sources that measurement and assignation took place in 122 and 121 around Carthage. It is thus certain that there was centuriated land in the region of Carthage, and perhaps beyond, before the end of the second century, and the only question is the identity of the centuriation of the sources with the remains on the ground. In fact, a difficulty arises. If a large section of the province was centuriated shortly after the conquest, it is not likely that the *groma* would have been planted in the Byrsa, in the middle of the land so recently laid under a solemn curse by Scipio Aemilianus. Yet it is hardly conceivable that two axes should meet on the Byrsa by sheer coincidence.[22] This dilemma can be solved in one of the three following ways, though none is wholly satisfactory. It may be that centuriation started in the north and that the centuriation around Carthage, while having the same orientation, that of sunrise at summer solstice, does not share the same axes but was laid out fresh by C. Gracchus and his helpers. This should be subject to verification.[23] A second possibility is to see the Gracchan scheme as extending far beyond Carthage. Generous allotments to 6000 settlers would in fact have necessitated this, yet would not account for the thousands of square kilometers of the northern group of centuriations.[24] The third option is to suppose that any centuriation of the second century vanished without trace beneath another subsequent one. Since it is long use rather than the initial laying out which preserves a centuriated landscape, this last is not impossible, but the complete disappearance of an earlier pattern on a different orientation is nevertheless unlikely. The conclusion seems to be that the northern group of centuriations may indeed have been laid out over a long period of time, but with a common orientation and perhaps common axes. The work around Carthage, including the implantation of the *groma* on the Byrsa, is most likely to be that of Gracchus, given the inscription and the implication in the ancient sources that he touched accursed soil, which probably meant the whole peninsula of Carthage.

Proof however is admittedly lacking, and while the 200-*iugera* unit used is typical for Gracchan land allotments it is equally common later.[25] The situation would be much more satisfactory if a few sites of second century date could be located in undoubted relation to the squares, for instance at the corners or in the centers. Alternatively, if it could be shown that a foot of 0.295 meter was used for the rural centuriation and one of 0.294 meter for the urban grid, this would be good evidence for a lapse of time between the two.

Along with his measurement and assignation, Gracchus also effected the growth of the political idea that the provinces were to be exploited for the benefit of the Roman people, and thus took a step along the road that led to the view that sovereignty might be equated with ownership of the soil. From then on the idea of assigning land overseas was firmly imprinted in the Roman mind as the mark of a "popular" political line, one which ignored the traditional authority of the senate in favor of methods more directly relying on the wishes and the sovereign power of the Roman people.[26]

The allotment of land in Africa was a particularly sensitive issue. While not actually active at Carthage, Marius visited the site and was responsible, as a result of his brief alliance with the popular politician Saturninus, for the allotment of land elsewhere in the province.[27] An inscription shows that the father of Julius Caesar was involved in part of this, if the site mentioned is correctly interpreted as the islands of Kerkennah.[28] Pompey, on the other hand, when working for Sulla, solemnly renewed the ritual curse.[29] A land bill of 64 B.C. that aimed at distributing overseas land was defeated; among its instigators was probably Julius Caesar.[30] Thus Caesar's eventual proposal to colonize the site of Carthage after the civil wars was not simply a practical solution to the problem of landless veteran soldiers and poor citizens, nor was it even a desire to revitalize a site of economic potential too great to be ignored. Caesar, as rival of Pompey and inheritor of the "popular" tradition of Gracchus through Marius, took a decision of great political import and even symbolic significance. *Pontifex maximus* since 63 B.C., he had nevertheless already in his notorious consulship of 59 B.C. shown himself quite ready to flout religious ritual when it obstructed politics. Who then more likely to decide, not simply to colonize Carthage, but to plant a new city on top of the accursed Carthaginian one? The story that he dreamed, while near Carthage, of a mob of veterans and poor citizens imploring him for land, while it may be entirely fictitious, was of good propaganda value and implied that the gods now favored the scheme.[31] But can it be determined what Caesar actually did?

An often received view is that he did little beyond taking a decision in principle. In fact the case for actual settlement in 44, just subsequent to Caesar's death or even before it, with operations most probably under the immediate supervision of Statilius Taurus, is convincing.[32] Even so, it has been argued that any Caesarian colonists were in fact settled, not on the site of the Punic city, but to one side of it, on ground that was less obviously accursed, namely the area of La Malga.[33] The arguments demand examination.

The first rests on the fact that the oldest known cemetery of Roman Carthage was discovered at Bir ez-Zitoun, near the amphitheater and the La Malga cisterns. But even given the possibility that the burials go back to pre-Augustan times (which on published evidence is not necessarily the case) the location of this cemetery looks as if it was simply determined by the exit road prolonging the *decumanus maximus*.[34] No conclusions over the site of the pre-Augustan city seem justified. In second place comes the discovery near the La Malga cisterns of the two famous reliefs of which one is now in Algiers, the other in the Louvre. One shows a mythological scene connected with the fertility of the earth, very close in subject and style to one on the Ara Pacis at Rome. The other shows Venus Genetrix with her son, a helmeted Mars in the middle, and a togate figure usually interpreted as Divus Julius (it certainly bears no resemblance to him as he is portrayed before deification).[35] Clearly some important monument of Augustan date but connected with Caesar, whether altar or temple, had stood in this area of the city, and the choice of site may be thought to require explanation. A contrast between this site and that of the altar to the *gens Augusta* found on the Byrsa is however invalidated by the fact that the latter was explicitly erected in private ground by private initiative.[36] To conclude that the center of the Julian city lay near La Malga, much less that it was laid out on the rural centuriation, is stretching the evidence. As for the discovery in the same area of the inscription of the *III viri* of 121, although it could well have been recut or copied, its position is most likely to be explained by the intersection in this area of the limits of the rural centuries.[37]

The final argument sometimes adduced, that Caesar hesitated to order the implantation of his colony on top of the heart of the accursed Punic city, totally lacks cogency, the more so as it is universally admitted that the area of La Malga would be included within the curse. Such hesitation, and the implied "temporary" solution of a city that did not face the sea, would be quite out of character. Only a failure of nerve on the part of Statilius Taurus, or insufficient time to prepare the ground nearer the sea, could explain a choice of site other than that of the actual future city. Conceivably, however, the ruinous and uneven nature of the ground along the coast favored initial building on a peripheral site less littered with remains of the Punic city, and thus in practice further inland.

That actual building took place is implied in various ways by the ancient sources. Statilius Taurus is accredited with the erection of *moenia* (buildings, not city walls), Lepidus found something to destroy (whether because he objected on religious grounds or for some other political reason).[38] The refoundation by Augustus in 29 B.C. consisted of a strengthening, possibly combined with certain constitutional changes, and obviously led to further building.[39] More conscious than his adopted father that the whole scheme required justification in the eyes of many Romans, Augustus was fortunate in having the poet Vergil to hand. Although the actual observations which went into Vergil's description of the nascent Carthage have little to do with that city, the psychological connection with the new Roman Carthage is obvious, and it is in effect a Roman city that is described.[40]

Where however does the actual street plan of Roman Carthage fit into this story? A distinction must clearly be drawn between a decision to colonize on a particular spot, the official *deductio* of colonists attended by religious ceremonies, the laying out of a preconceived street plan, and finally the actual building of houses and monuments in accordance with it. It has been argued above that the decision to site the new Carthage above the Punic one was that of Julius Caesar. Archaeological evidence can by its nature only attest the latest part of the process, and it is thus not surprising if it currently suggests an Augustan or even Tiberian date for actual urbanization.[41] A delay is in any case only to be expected in the completion of such ambitious projects as the monumental leveling operations on the Byrsa (which incidentally would destroy the original location of the *groma*, since the original summit of the hill was removed).

A more detailed examination of the street plan is desirable in order to see if the authorship can be determined. The most striking feature is of course the extreme regularity observed over so wide an area. It is hardly surprising that the natives of Roman Carthage were proud of their wide straight avenues, which singled them out from so many other African towns and were a fitting symbol of the city's preeminence.[42] But there are other respects besides size and regularity in which the plan of Carthage is no ordinary one, and remains without precise parallel. Each *insula* measures 120 by 480 Roman feet, that is one by four linear *actus*, and four square *actus* comprise 2 *iugera* or one *heredium*, precisely one hundredth part of the big rural centuries and by long tradition the original land allotment of the most ancient Romans. Moreover, the *insulae* are arranged in four quarters by the intersecting main axes. If ever a street plan deserved the application of the terms *cardo* and *decumanus*, actually only attested for rural *limitatio*, it is that of Carthage. Although doubt may be expressed as to which is really which—a *decumanus* was normally east to west, but might also run parallel to the sea—it is hard to avoid using the terms, or to suppose that they would be avoided.[43] That the four quarters of the city do not form square centuries of 200 *iugera*, corresponding precisely to the rural ones, is due to the fact that the roads were not included within the measured *insulae* but were added outside them, in the fashion described by the legal formula *iter populo non debetur*.[44] Nevertheless, each quarter conforms exactly to another type of century, the *centuria strigata* of 240 *iugera* (2,800 × 3,000 ft.), and it is this fact rather than any archaeological evidence which proves Saumagne correct.

All this adds up to the fact that we have here a plan very carefully devised by a planner who was familiar with the whole tradition of Roman land measuring, capable of combining to an extraordinary degree practical and theoretical considerations. The long narrow *insulae*, more reminiscent of Greek than Roman city plans, yet corresponding to Roman measurements, may have been suggested by the major slope of the land toward the coast.[45] The chosen orientation was probably determined by three factors. The first was the desire to avoid the midday sun shining directly down the streets as would have happened if the line of the rural centuriation had been followed. The second was to have the streets roughly parallel to the shore, and the third, dramatically revealed by the recent German excavations, was the desire to reutilize certain remains of the Hellenistic Punic city, part of which already lay on this orientation.[46]

The one exception to the regularity of the plan is of course the missing northwest corner, cut off by the line which delimits the rural centuriation one century northwest of the Byrsa. Usually interpreted as Augustan respect for a preexisting Caesarian colony, it is, if the foregoing arguments are right, much more likely to be respect for the Gracchan centuriation or perhaps, indeed, for the Gracchan city that never came to be—in any case a symbolic reminder of the anteriority of the Gracchan scheme. Such a gesture of respect, it can be argued, is more to be expected of Caesar than of Augustus. The argument is however hardly conclusive, nor are the others which can be adduced.

It may of course be objected that the use of the *actus* of 120 feet was too common to deserve remark. In fact, although the linear *actus* was frequently used, *insulae* measuring an exact number of square *actus* are by no means common, nor is the maintenance of the same set of measurements throughout a whole city plan. The closest known parallel to Carthage is Iader in Dalmatia, where some of the *insulae* at least may have been exactly as at Carthage: there is of course no comparison in the grandeur of the cities. Unfortunately, Iader too may have been either a Caesarian or an Augustan foundation, though the later date is usually preferred.[47] The plan of Carthage may also be compared and contrasted with that of Turin, another that is remarkable for its uniformity and this time certainly an Augustan foundation. Here the *insulae* also appear to measure four square *actus*, but they are square, and the plan lacks the strong axiality of Carthage as well as its size. Aosta, though in some ways like Turin, had rectangular *insulae* not expressable in square *actus*, although the plan in its entirety does form an exact number.[48]

What may be said without fear of contradiction is that the Carthage plan reflects its age. The period of Caesar and Augustus saw a great renewal of agrimensorial activity, required by the allotment of land and the foundation of colonies throughout the empire.[49] We know little of the individuals involved, apart from one of Caesar's surveyors, a Spaniard, who was promoted to be tribune of the plebs and drew from Cicero the sarcastic comment that his behavior suggested he wanted to measure out Rome itself as if it were a colony.[50] Some outstanding practitioner of the art dreamed up the plan of Carthage, but who he was, and for which master he worked, cannot be known with certainty. The agrimensorial tradition has much to say about what it owed to both Caesar and Augustus. Ultimately, whether the inspiration for the plan be attributed to the *celeritas* of Caesar or to the thoughtfulness of his heir must remain a matter for debate. Moreover no help can be derived from the attested name of the colony, Colonia Iulia Concordia Karthago, which could equally be Caesarian or Augustan.[51] It can at least be claimed that there is no overwhelming weight of evidence against attributing the idea to Caesar, even if Augustus had to carry it out: and, except for the doubts occasioned by other features in Appian's account, it would be tempting to suppose that it might have been instructions for the street plan that were discovered in the dead dictator's papers.[52]

One final point: it has been suggested that the Roman's determination to subject African soil to the Roman imprint of centuriation was partly the result of the fear and suspicion engendered by that strange land out of which new monstrosities were always proverbially supposed to arise.[53] The magnificent regularity of the street grid is surely to be placed in the same tradition. One of the finest fruits of the Roman tradition of land measuring and town planning, it symbolizes both the Romanity and the grandeur of the city reborn on accursed soil after one hundred years of political and ideological strife.

NOTES

1. Ch. Saumagne, "Colonia Iulia Karthago," *BAC,* 1924, pp. 131–39; P. Davin, "Etude sur la cadastration de la Colonia Julia Carthago," *RevTun,* 1930, pp. 74–85. The most readily accessible plan is the scaled-down reproduction of Davin's in F. Castagnoli, *Orthogonal Town Planning in Antiquity* (Cambridge, Mass., 1971), p. 114 (see frontispiece above).

2. Theoretically the precise measurements using the foot of 0.294 m should be 42.34 m, 7.06 m, and 35.28 m respectively, and the length from center road to center road of the *decumani* should be 148.18 m. In "Les recherches récentes sur la topographie de Carthage," *JSav,* 1931, pp. 145–57, Saumagne pays tribute to Davin but quotes figures of 42.50 and 148.30 approximately.

3. J. W. Eadie and J. H. Humphrey, "The Topography of the Southeast Quarter of Later Roman Carthage," *Excavations at Carthage Conducted by the University of Michigan, 1976,* vol. 3, ed. J. H. Humphrey (Ann Arbor, 1977), p. 2.

4. From center to center of *decumani* is on this basis 148.68 m. On the varying value of the Roman foot see O. A. W. Dilke, *The Roman Land Surveyors* (Newton Abbot, 1971), pp. 82–85. Since the Carthage streets grew progressively narrower with time, it is in practice hard to discover the original width.

5. S. Lancel, J. Deneauve, J. M. Carrié, "Le Cardo Maximus et les édifices situés à l'est de la voie (secteur C)," *AntAfr* 11 (1977): 107. Theoretically the width of the *cardo maximus* should be 11.76 or 11.80 m, if it was intended to be 40 ft.

6. For this and other subsequently mentioned information concerning the Italian sector, see the brief report by A. Carandini in *CEDAC Bulletin* 1 (September 1978): 16–17. Professor Carandini has kindly informed me that the junction between *cardo* II west and *decumanus* IV north was in fact a T-junction, since *cardo* II south of the junction had not been built up.

7. See the report by C. M. Wells and E. M. Wightman in *JFA* 7(1980): 43–63. It should be noted that on the general plan (fig. 3-1) the theoretical street grid has been extended for clarity's sake up to and when appropriate beyond *decumanus* VI, even at points where it has not been confirmed by excavation.

8. Some earlier layers below and adjacent may form the remains of earlier road surfaces largely destroyed in the building of the later one: their nature is at present not entirely clear. See Wells and Wightman, *JFA* 7(1980): 43–63.

9. That the Teurf el-Sour might be of artificial origin was suggested by H. Hurst, "Excavations at Carthage 1974: First Interim Report," *AntJ* 55 (1975): 37.

10. "Carte archéologique et topographique des ruines de Carthage dressée d'après les relevés de M. l'adjoint du Génie Bordy avec le concours de MM. R. P. Delattre, le Général Dolot, P. Gauckler: autorisierte Nachbildung aus dem Atlas archéologique de la Tunisie Massstab 1:16,000," in *RE* 10: opp. cols. 2, 159–60.

11. H. Hurst, "Excavations at Carthage 1974," p. 35. See also the comments by Eadie and Humphrey in *Michigan, 1976*, vol. 3, p. 2.

12. H. Hurst, "Excavations at Carthage 1975: Second Interim Report," *AntJ* 56 (1976): 193–4.

13. See report in *JFA* 7(1980): 43–63, or more briefly, C. M. Wells and E. M. Wightman, "Carthage 1978: la muraille Théodosienne," *Classical News and Views* 23 (1979): 17.

14. A. Audollent, *Carthage romaine: 146 avant Jésus-Christ–698 après Jésus-Christ* (Paris, 1901), pp. 56 and 183, in fact connected aqueduct and cisterns and thus inclined toward a second century date for the latter. The idea that the cisterns might belong to the Caesarian colony is due to St. Gsell, "Les premiers temps de la Carthage romaine," *RHist* 154–56 (1927): 235. Gsell tried to incorporate them into his view of a Caesarian colony adopting the lines of the rural cadastration in the area of La Malga. Though based on no archaeological evidence, the idea has since then been often quoted.

15. For this unpublished information and permission to use it here I am grateful to Professor Carandini and his team.

16. The work on the cadastrations is essentially that of Saumagne, "Colonia Iulia Karthago." The meeting point of the grids is most precisely described by Davin, "La cadastration de la Colonia Julia Carthago," p. 80, "Le *groma*... tombe dans l'intérieur et au chevet de la Cathédrale actuelle, sensiblement dans son axe." Gsell, "Les premiers temps de la Carthage romaine," pp. 225–40 made sense of the literary sources and, in particular, disentangled the slightly confusing evidence on Caesarian and Augustan foundations and the part played by Statilius Taurus as Caesar's legate. His reconstruction has gained complete acceptance: see, e.g., J. Carcopino, "L'Afrique au dernier siècle de la république romaine," *RHist* 162 (1929): 86–95. P. Romanelli, *Storia delle province Romane dell'Africa* (Rome, 1959), p. 137.

17. An exception is L. Teutsch, *Das römische Städtewesen in Nordafrika,* (Berlin, 1962), p. 3 n.12, who points out the lack of proof.

18. The story of the wolves is told most fully by Plut. *C. Gracch.* 11 and Appian *B Civ.* 1. 24. 4, but is also found more briefly in Julius Obsequens 33.

19. Both Plutarch and Appian talk of city boundaries, while Julius Obsequens explicitly mentions field boundaries (*limites qui in agrorum divisione... depositi erant*).

20. *CIL* 8. 12535, and for a commentary, C. Cichorius, *Römische Studien* (Leipzig and Berlin, 1922), pp. 113–16. For the *lex agraria*, Riccobono, *FIRA*[2] 1: 102–21. Its application to Carthage is fully discussed in J. Carcopino, *Autour des Gracques*, 2d ed. (Paris, 1967), p. 129. The *lex agraria* 66 and 90 refers to existing centuries in Africa, whereas in 97 the territory of Corinth is still *metiundum*.

21. The arguments are summarized by R. Chevallier, "Essai de chronologie des centuriations romaines de Tunisie," *MelRome* 70 (1958): 61–128.

22. Ibid., p. 65. calls attention to this problem, but does not succeed in resolving it.

23. The *Atlas des centuriations romaines de la Tunisie* (Paris, 1954) was not available to me at the time of writing. An examination of the *Carte de Tunisie au 50,000ᵉ* for the neighborhood of Carthage suggested the possibility that some lines in the immediate vicinity might have been very slightly modified to obtain the crossing of axes on the Byrsa.

24. This is argued by Carcopino, *Autour des Gracques* and idem, "L'Afrique au dernier siècle de la république romaine," pp. 86–95.

25. *Gromatici veteres* ed. Lachmann, 136 and 209 show that the Gracchi were commonly associated with the 200-*iugera* century. Cf. the reference to 200 *iugera* as the maximum that might be held by a single owner of African soil in the *lex agraria* 60 (Riccobono, *FIRA*² 1: 102–21). See also Dilke, *Roman Land Surveyors*, p. 134.

26. For a recent discussion of the development of the notion of "ownership" of provincial soil, see J. Bleicken, "'In provinciali solo dominium populi Romani est vel Caesaris'. Zur Kolonisationspolitik der ausgehenden Republik and frühen Kaiserzeit," *Chiron* 4 (1974): 359–414.

27. Velleius 2. 19. 4, Plut. *Mar.* 40. For Marius's distributions of land, Appian *B Civ.* 1. 29. 130, Plut. *Crass.* 2. 10 (no mention of Africa).

28. T. Frank, "The New *Elogium* of Caesar's Father," *AJP* 58 (1937): 90–93. The identification with Kerkennah, where Marius once took refuge (Plut. *Mar.* 40) is accepted by P. Brunt, *Italian Manpower* (Oxford, 1971), p. 577, but rejected in favor of Mariana in Corsica by T. D. Barnes, "A Marian Colony," *CR* 21 (1971): 332.

29. This can be inferred from the specific mention of *trinas Pompei aras* in Tert. *de pallio* 1. Plutarch, while mentioning Pompey's sojourn in Carthage, where his army fell to treasure hunting, makes no such reference. What Pompey actually did is however of less importance in this context than what he was believed to have done.

30. Cic. *Leg. Agr.* 1. 25 made capital from the fact that the law would have allowed allotments at Carthage. Carcopino, *Jules César* (Paris, 1969), pp. 147–48, argues strongly for the view that Caesar was behind the Sullan land bill.

31. Appian *Punica* 136 for Caesar's dream, where however it is implied that Caesar did not actually manage to send out colonists. Dio 43. 50. 3–4 and Plut. *Caes.* 57 talk of actual foundations by Caesar, as does Strabo 17. 3. 15 and Pausan. 2. 1. 2.

32. See n. 31 for clear references to a Caesarian foundation. The Tertullian passage *de pallio* 1. 2 (*CSEL* vol. 76, p. 105) is capable of more than one interpretation and has provoked discussion accordingly. Referring to the granting of Roman citizenship to Carthage, it reads in full, "*Post Gracchi obscena omina et Lepidi violenta ludibria, post trinas Pompei aras et longas Caesaris moras, ubi moenia*

Statilius Taurus imposuit, sollemnia Sentius Saturninus enarravit, cum Concordia Iulia (an emendation for mss. cum concordia iuvat) *toga oblata est."* The activities of Statilius Taurus can be linked to his attested presence in Africa in 36 B.C. (Dio 49. 14). Alternatively they can be bracketed with the ceremonies held by Sentius Saturninus: these are usually connected with Octavian's despatching of further colonists to Carthage, dated to 29 B.C. by Dio 52. 43. 1. While the passage in a general way indicates a date after Caesar's death for the foundation of the colony, its compressed rhetorical style avoids precision, and the textual corruption does not help. Gsell, "Les premiers temps de la Carthage romaine," argues convincingly that the reference to Taurus is best linked with the firm date of 44 B.C. (the consulship of Anthony and Dolabella) provided by Solinus 27. 11 (and also implied by Appian *Libyca* 136) and that a legateship of Statilius Taurus in that year rather than his activity in Africa in 36 (Dio 49. 14) was to be seen as the occasion. Supporting evidence is given by Cic. *Fam.* 12. 25. 1. which shows that Statilius Taurus was, as a supporter of the superseded Caesarian governor Calvisius, closely involved in a dispute over the governorship of Africa in 43 B.C. Carcopino, in "L'Afrique au dernier siècle de la république romaine," accepted Gsell's reconstruction but felt that the tradition of Caesar's foundation was so strong in the sources (with the exception of Appian) that it suggested a date just prior to his murder, i.e., in the consulship of Caesar and Antony. The sources consistently stress the analogy between Carthage and Corinth, destroyed in the same year and also colonized by Caesar.

33. Gsell, "Les premiers temps de la Carthage romaine," p. 233.

34. A. Delattre, "Les cimetières romains superposés de Carthage," *RA*, 1898, pp. 82–101. Some of the stones may well belong to the last decades B.C., but in the absence of illustrations of the pottery it is impossible to arrive at a more precise date. Chevallier, in "Des centuriations romaines de Tunisie," seems to confuse this cemetery with other early burials to the northwest of Sidi Bou Said. The reference here seems to be to the burials discussed by Delattre in *Les lampes antiques du musée de Saint-Louis de Carthage* (Lille, 1889), pp. 6–7, where neither the exact position nor the date is clear.

35. The discovery of the stones was reported in *RAfr* 1 (1856–57): 490, and 2 (1857–58): 327. They are discussed by Gsell, "Les statues du temple de Mars Ultor à Rome," *RA*, 1899, 37–43; by M. Rostovtzeff, "Augustus," *RomMitt* 38–40 (1923–24): 294; by S. Weinstock, "Pax and the Ara Pacis," *JRS* 50 (1960): 54–55. The Altar to the gens *Augusta* is reported by Cagnat in *CRAI*, 1913, p. 680; cf. V. Ehrenberg, A. H. M. Jones, *Documents Illustrating the Reigns of Augustus and Tiberius* 2d ed. (Oxford, 1955), no. 135.

36. I.e., it need hardly have been in a Caesarian forum, as suggested by Chevallier, "Des centuriations de Tunisie."

37. Gsell, in "Les premiers temps de la Carthage romaine," betrays a certain lack of ease with his own arguments at this point. The tradition in Appian *Libyca* 2 and 136 that Roman Carthage was near, not on, the Punic site

specifically refers to the Augustan foundation, and is also patently false. It may represent an attempt at propaganda.

38. Tert. *de pallio* 1; Dio 52. 43. 1. Why Lepidus's destruction should have been thought to abrogate the colonists' rights has never been satisfactorily explained.

39. Dio 52. 43: 3,000 Italians were sent and some indigenous people included. For a discussion of the full name (Colonia Iulia Concordia Karthago) and constitution Teutsch, *Städtewesen,* p. 103. *Chron. min.,* ed. Mommsen 1. 217 and 276 seem to refer to a refoundation, which they take as the true foundation, in the year 28 B.C., with respective entries *"Carthago libertatem a populo Romano recepit"* and *"Chartago restituta est idus Iulias."* The wording is strange and, like the Tertullian passage, has given rise to various interpretations: see discussion in Teutsch, *Städtewesen,* p. 158, where their reliability is questioned.

40. Vergil *Aen.* 1. 365. See Carcopino, *Virgile et les origines d'Ostie,* 2d ed. (Paris, 1968), p. 750.

41. J. Humphrey, "North African Newsletter 1," *AJA* 82 (1978): 516–17.

42. *Expositio totius mundi* 61, *geog. lat. min.* ed. Riese 123; Pomp. Mel. 1.7. 34.

43. J. de Gall, "Rites de fondation," *BSAF,* 1970, pp. 292–307 and "Les romains et l'orientation solaire," *MelRomeA* 87 (1975): 287–320 argues that *cargo, decumanus,* and solar orientation were virtually never applied to towns, though there were some exceptions such as Ammaedara (*Gromatici veteres* ed. Lachmann, 180). F. Castagnoli, *Orthogonal Town Planning,* p. 115, suggests that the *decumanus maximus* would more probably be laid out parallel to the coastline than at right angles to it.

44. Explained by Saumagne, "Colonia Iulia Karthago," with reference to *Gromatici veteres* ed. Lachmann 293. See also Saumagne, "Iter populo non debetur," *RevPhil* 3d. ser. 2 (1928): 320–52.

45. J. B. Ward-Perkins, *Cities of Ancient Greece and Italy* (London, 1974), p. 28.

46. Short report by F. Rakob in *CEDAC* 1: 6.

47. Castagnoli, *Orthogonal Town Planning,* p. 115. On the date of Iader, P. Brunt, *Italian Manpower* (Oxford, 1971), p. 597. J. J. Wilkes, *Dalmatia* (London, 1970), p. 206, attributes it firmly to Augustus.

48. Castagnoli, *Orthogonal Town Planning,* pp. 110–13.

49. Dilke, *Roman Land Surveyors,* p. 37: Gromatici veteres ed. Lachmann 394–95.

50. Cic. *Phil.* 11. 2 and 14. 10.

51. See the discussions by C. van Nerom, "Colonia Iulia Concordia Karthago," in *Hommages à M. Renard* (Brussels, 1969), 2: 767–76 (where however the evidence for Statilius Taurus is ignored) and B. Galsterer-Kröll, "Untersuchungen zu den Beinamen der Städte des Imperium Romanum," *Epigraphische Studien* 9, (1972): 66–67.

52. Appian *Punica* 136. Appian's tradition, while different and on the

whole less trustworthy than that of Dio, nevertheless has an inner coherence which might point to a misunderstood source or an alternative tradition rather than a sheer muddle. There is a hint of Caesar's customary *celeritas* in Dio. 43. 14. 1.

53. Audollent, "Carthage romaine," p. 3. Plin. *NH* 8. 17 (42) *unde etiam vulgare Graeciae dictum semper aliquid novi Africam adferre.*

IV. The Defense of Carthage

C. M. Wells

The natural strength of the site of Carthage, which so impressed ancient writers, was far more apparent in antiquity than today, when the silting-up of the bays on either side has blurred the original outline of the peninsula on which Carthage stands.[1] How formidable Carthage was, with the advantages of the site reinforced by the most sophisticated military engineering of its time, can be divined from the accounts of the operations of Hellenistic and Roman generals, who struck at the supply routes linking Carthage to the interior, captured on occasion Tunis, Utica, or Bizerta, but dared not attack or made little headway against Carthage itself.

The descriptions which we have of the defenses of late Punic Carthage testify better to the impression that they made on contemporaries than to the latters' powers of observation and precise description. Strabo's figure of nearly 64 kilometers for the total length of the defenses is rightly suspect: the same figure is given for the defenses of Babylon, and the coincidence is probably not coincidental.[2] Other sources suggest, more reasonably, a figure half Strabo's, around 32 kilometers,[3] which is still high, compared with 18 kilometers for the total circuit of the Aurelian Wall at Rome,[4] at a time when Rome's population will have been more than double that of Carthage and much more than double that of Punic Carthage. Even Dionysius I's great fortifications at Syracuse, taking in the heights of Epipolae, were only 27 kilometers long.

Appian, whose version goes back to that of the eyewitness Polybius, says that Carthage was surrounded by a single wall, within which the naval harbor had its own circuit of defenses, with a triple wall on the landward side of the city. Each of the three walls was 13.32 meters high, not counting battlements and towers, and 8.88 meters wide, with towers and bastions every 59 meters, and contained stables for elephants and

horses, and barracks for men.[5] There must also have been catapult platforms: Carthage surrendered 2,000 catapults to the Romans in 146 B.C.[6]
Despite some scholars' scepticism—Sznycer, the most recent writer on
the subject, would reduce the triple wall to a ditch with a palisade and
two ramparts[7]—I do not see why there should not in fact have been three
separate lines of fortification cutting off the city on the landward side,
where it was obviously most vulnerable. We should not be surprised if
Carthage had such elaborate defenses, when we consider what fortifications many lesser Hellenistic cities went in for. Professor Lancel's paper
in this volume reminds us how strong the Hellenistic influence was on
late Punic Carthage, and Hellenistic fortifications were highly developed:

> From the fifth century onward almost every town had been enclosed
> by a strong wall of great length, joined to a still more formidable
> citadel. The approaches from the frontier also called for protection. In
> all, the Greeks built many thousands of miles of fortifications, and
> every successive improvement in siegecraft compelled a degree of
> modernization. . . . Expenditure upon defence restricted most of the
> Greek states in other forms of public works.[8]

For all the interest these Punic defenses have attracted, remarkably
little is really known about them. Even General Duval's claim to have
partially traced from the air and subsequently excavated a line of Punic
defenses going north across the isthmus from the Lake of Tunis, in itself
not implausible, does not appear from the published evidence capable of
sustaining all that has been built upon it.[9] Reyniers, for instance, elabo-
rates it into a hypothesis of three sets of defenses: Duval's outer circuit,
then those of the city itself, with Appian's triple wall on the landward
side, and finally those of Byrsa.[10] But this remains a hypothesis, while
Lapeyre's supposed Punic defenses of Byrsa have been shown by the
current French excavators on the Byrsa to be nothing of the sort.[11]

The defense of the Carthage peninsula and of the city itself is however linked with the measures taken at different times to secure the
whole region against attack, especially attack by the native highlanders to
the west. Rome's eventual solution to the defense of Carthage was to
remove any threat of attack to a safe distance. At first, however, after the
capture and destruction of Carthage at the end of the Third Punic War in
146 B.C., Rome was content simply to delimit the territory taken over and
incorporated in the new Roman province of Africa; the boundary between the new province and the kingdom of Numidia, the so-called
King's Ditch, the *fossa regia,* was still the boundary between the provinces

of Africa *vetus* and Africa *nova* over 200 years later (fig. 4-1).[12] Some scholars have wished to see the *fossa regia* as a defensive barrier, not merely an administrative limit, but this is anachronistic.[13] No more in Africa than in Gaul was there a connected linear frontier at this time, and the Numidians were clients who played the role, beyond the provincial limits, which the Aedui, for instance, played in Gaul. Not until later, when the forward impetus of their republican imperialism was exhausted, did the Romans seek to stabilize and defend frontiers with a *limes*-type barrier and the garrisons along it which alone would give it meaning.[14]

During the century or so which followed the destruction of Carthage, Africa was in many ways a backwater. Jugurtha showed what a menace to Roman interests an ambitious native ruler could be. But for much of the time it is hard to resist what Desanges calls

> l'impression qu'entre l'époque de Carthage et celle de l'Empire romain, l'Afrique a traversé une morte-saison. Nos connaissances se sont renouvelées ici à un rhythme moins vif qu'ailleurs, et les deux tomes consacrés, il y a un demi-siècle, par Gsell... à l'Afrique romaine, de 146 à 27 avant notre ère, sont assurément ceux qui appellent le moins de retouches.[15]

The triumviral period and the early years of Augustus brought renewed activity. Five generals triumphed *ex Africa* in fifteen years: L. Statilius Taurus in 34 B.C., L. Cornificius in 33, L. Autronius Paetus in 28, L. Sempronius Atratinus in 21, and L. Cornelius Balbus (the last triumph by a man outside the imperial house) in 19. Two other generals received the *ornamenta triumphalia* a generation later: L. Passienus Rufus in A.D. 3, and Cn. Cornelius Lentulus Cossus, henceforth surnamed Gaetulicus, in A.D. 6, along with King Juba. The result of all this fighting was to extend Roman control in the south and southwest of the province,[16] thus improving the security of the Roman settlers further north, at Carthage and elsewhere, by pushing further away the zone susceptible to razzias from the desert tribes. Juba's realm was an essential part of the system. Suetonius tells us that Augustus treated his client kings as *membra partesque imperii*.[17] Juba, *rex et socius*, flaunting the ornaments of a Roman triumph, is little different from a provincial governor of a small and backward province.

The security of the province suffered a setback with the revolt of Tacfarinas, which broke out in A.D. 17. Tacitus's characteristic topographical vagueness has made this episode the delight of scholars. The great nineteenth-century scholars assumed that Tebessa (Theveste), west of the present Algerian-Tunisian border, was already a legionary base from the time of Augustus onward. A masterly article by de Pachtère, however, written on active service before Salonica and published in 1916,[18] argued that Tebessa became the base only under Vespasian, and that Haïdra (Ammaedara) was the legionary base at the end of Augustus's reign and throughout the Julio-Claudian period. The strategic importance of the Haïdra region cannot be denied. Haïdra itself lies on the road from Carthage to Tebessa where it is joined by a second road coming west from Sousse (Hadrumetum) via Sbiba (Sufes) and Thala. Milestones apparently dating from A.D. 14 record the building of yet another road from Gabes (Tacapae) via Gafsa (Capsa) to the *castra hiberna*, apparently some 150 kilometers further on (a distance which, *pace* de Pachtère, suits equally well the Haïdra region or Tebessa).[19] It is probably right to see this road as designed to "acheminer facilement et rapidement des renforts venus en Africa par mer et débarqués dans les ports de la Petite Syrte, jusqu'au coeur meme d'une zone qui s'était révélée dangereuse au début du siècle."[20] This zone was centered on Haïdra (see fig. 4-1).

The importance of Haïdra in the military communications network is further stressed by the building under Justinian, at a time when conditions of insecurity in this area had reverted to those prevailing at the beginning of the first century A.D., of a new fortress at Haïdra to guard the road junction and the bridge across the Oued Haïdra, linking it with a system of watchtowers and bastions, including one created out of the arch of Septimius Severus at the eastern entrance to the city.[21] On the other hand, no trace of military installations of the early empire has ever been found at Haïdra, and some of the evidence is difficult to reconcile with de Pachtère's theory. For instance, Tacitus relates that at the end of the summer of 22, Blaesus, in the war against Tacfarinas, decided for the first time not to winter his army in the old province ("nec, ut mos fuerat, acta aestate retrahit copias aut in hibernaculis veteris provinciae componit"[22]). Since Haïdra lies outside the old province, as delimited by the *fossa regia*, this would seem to exclude Haïdra as a permanent legionary base before 22 at the earliest. De Pachtère, pointing out that a slave of the household of Cornelius Cethegus (proconsul about 30)[23] was buried at Haïdra, argues that Haïdra must then have been the legionary headquarters, but even if this is so the permanent headquarters were perhaps established there only after the suppression of Tacfarinas's revolt in 24.

Perhaps the search for a single legionary base before this, at Haïdra or elsewhere, is in fact misconceived. This was guerrilla warfare. In 22, the army was divided. Blaesus, commanding in the central sector, which included the Haïdra area, established "castella et munitiones idoneis locis," no doubt like the one we hear of two years earlier at Thala some 20 kilometers east of Haïdra, the scene of a notable exploit by the "gregarius miles," Helvius Rufus.[24] Nor had legionary bases yet evolved into the stereotyped permanent "fortresses" of the Flavian and later periods.[25] Possibly at Augustan Haltern in Germany,[26] certainly at Claudian-Neronian Longthorpe in Britain,[27] we find a base designed to accommodate less than a full legion. If there was a base in or near Haïdra, we should not necessarily expect an earlier Lambaesis. What is certain is that the wars in Africa under Augustus and the final defeat of Tacfarinas thoroughly pacified the crucial Haïdra area, advanced Roman control to the edge of the chotts in the south, and removed from all further danger of attack by the nomadic tribesmen the fertile plains to the north, and *a fortiori* Carthage, their capital.

The work of pacification, with all the implications that *pax* and *pacare* have in the early Empire ("tanta barbaria est ut nec intellegant pacem"),[28] thereafter moved west. Under Caligula, civil and military responsibility were divided, which can have been feasible only if the civil and military zones were *de facto* reasonably separate.[29] The later move of the headquarters of the legion to Tebessa under Vespasian, a move typical of his policy in frontier areas, and subsequently to Lambaesis effectively left Carthage in no more contact with the army and in no greater danger from possible attack than Rome itself. It was not of course wholly without a garrison. The proconsul of Africa had his own *singulares*—it would seem that both proconsul and legionary legate were entitled to their own personal guard after power was split and "aequatur inter eos beneficiorum numerus."[30] One cohort at a time was moreover detached from the legion at Lambaesis and stationed at Carthage "in officium proconsulis."[31] Carthage also had a *cohors urbana,* and Gauckler believed he had identified their barracks, occupied at least into the fourth century, if not later, on the summit of Bordj Djedid, an obvious site for such a unit, recalling that of the *castra praetoria* at Rome.[32]

During these centuries of peace, Carthage had no need of city walls. We need not invoke Rome's ancestral fear of Carthage to explain this, especially when we consider that Rome itself, until late in the third century, had no walls either. When danger threatened, then walls were built. In the case of Carthage, the date when the wall was built is given by the *Chronica Gallica* as 425;[33] it is commonly called the Theodosian Wall, after Theodosius II, then senior emperor. Now as Professor Clover has pointed out in one of the recent Michigan volumes on Carthage, the chronicle itself was written in 452 or soon after, and is generally reliable to within two to five years.[34] This would give us a date between 420 and 430 for the wall, and I would myself tend to accept Clover's suggested date of 423 to 425, though for reasons that appear to differ from his.

Clover in fact suggests that the wall was probably built "between 423 and 425, when an official named John usurped the throne of the West, briefly interrupting the sovereignty of the House of Theodosius, which at that time Boniface supported." Count Boniface became governor of Africa in 422 or 423. The wall has often been attributed to him ("l'hypothèse cadre bien avec ce que nous savons du caractère prudent et de la science militaire de Boniface," says Audollent),[35] and it seems reasonable to suppose that he put in hand this great work on taking up his responsibilities (new brooms sweep clean). It was, however, more probably inspired by fear of a barbarian invasion of Africa than by that of a precarious usurper. There is no doubt that the barbarian threat to Africa was fully appreciated by the imperial authorities. In 419 we find Honorius and Theodosius ordaining capital punishment for those who teach the barbarians how to build ships,[36] and a decision to wall Carthage fits well into this same pattern of imperial concern. We do not know how long the wall took to build. When Boniface himself, suspected of disloyalty, disobeyed a summons to the court of Ravenna, and imperial armies were sent against him, the second expedition under Sigisvult in 428 may actually have taken Carthage.[37] If so, this might suggest that it was not yet in a strong state of defense. But the evidence is inconclusive.

Whatever the precise date, a date for the building of the wall some time in the 420s suits the evidence from recent excavations. In the northern sector, the Italian excavations which have cut the wall west of the *cardo maximus*, and those of the second Canadian team east of it (directed by Professor Edith Wightman and myself) have produced, as we shall see, evidence consistent with such a dating, though nothing conclusive for it. But on the British site on the Avenue Bourguiba at Salammbo south of the city we have something firmer:

> The wall itself was cut into a ground level of stony loam containing eight fourth-century coins and a quantity of pottery of that date; a further three fourth-century coins were found in the body of the wall. The latest of these coins is of Honorius, giving the wall a *terminus post quem* of A.D. 400/423.[38]

The wall has of course been heavily robbed, and the process has been going on for a long time, continuing until quite recently, it would seem, if we can rely on evidence from our own site, which will be discussed. Beulé vividly described what was happening over a century ago: "Les Arabes ont jadis découvert cette muraille... Ils l'ont démolie pierre par pierre... il est resté un fossé large de près de quatre mètres."[39] How little was known of the wall before the current excavations began can be deduced from the extreme scantiness of Audollent's account,[40] and the absence of any section on the defenses from Colette Picard's survey of archaeological evidence from Carthage some thirty years ago.[41] Some local place names help to locate it, such as Bab el-Rih, the Gate of the Wind, the northern gate on the *cardo maximus*. Mediaeval Arab chroniclers tell us that the wall was bathed by the sea, that Saint Louis's army found the walls ruinous but still standing, that the Arab tribe of the Beni Ziad had built an earth rampart on the site[42]—an earth rampart that excavators in the early 1920s thought they had discovered, but wrongly, as we shall see later. We know that some areas were inside the wall (Henry Hodge has drawn attention to the implications of Procopius's account of Belisarius's attack in 533),[43] and others outside it, for instance Saint Cyprian's church[44] and the port installations which Audollent records between Sidi Bou Saïd and Bordj Djedid, "une série de petits abris pour les embarcations et de jetées relativement courtes."[45] Whether there were outlying fortifications to protect these installations is not known, but Humphrey and Eadie have recently noted evidence for one such outlying strongpoint south of the city toward the lake.[46]

The current excavations, however, have now added considerably to our knowledge both of the line of the Theodosian Wall and of its history and method of construction. Four teams have produced information about it: the Poles with their resistivity survey in the Douar Chott area, the British on the south side of the city, the Italians and the second Canadian team under Dr. Edith Wightman and myself on the north side along the Teurf el-Sour escarpment (see figs. 3-2, 3-4, 3-5). Evidence from the Polish survey is however very limited,[47] and the Italians have not yet published their results, save for a brief note in the first *CEDAC Bulletin*,[48] from which we learn that they have evidence consistent with the traditional date for the building of the wall, which obliterates some earlier graves. Close behind it, but separated by an impasse, military structures or habitations date from soon after the building of the wall. There is a mention in the report of "un mur nord-est/sud-ouest en liaison avec d'autres bâtiments (qui) paraît bien être une limite de camp" in the seventh century levels. Beyond the wall excavation showed that there was no ditch: "Le pendage naturel était une protection suffisante." The question is raised whether the slope which now coincides with the line of the wall is natural or artificial, but no clear answer is given (this is, as we shall see, a question that greatly interested us further east). The most interesting result is the absence of a ditch, which contrasts with what the British found on the south side, where the ground however is flat.

The British reports on their excavations are admirably complete and lucid. The report on the first season (1974) of excavations on the wall site is preceded by a résumé by Henry Hurst of previous knowledge of the wall, which begins by discussing the evidence of the *Chronica Gallica* and of Procopius, and then, noting that "The general course of the Theodosian Wall has for some time been postulated on the basis of features observed in the field," goes on to mention the "tour et poterne" on the northeast of the city excavated in the last century, the Teurf el-Sour and its continuation southward toward the La Malga cisterns, and various structures at La Malga which have been identified with the wall. From there "its suggested line . . . encompasses the cisterns, amphitheatre, circus, and the low hill Koudiat el Heurma" just west of the British site.[49]

The actual excavations on the British site revealed the wall to have been 3.5 meters wide, with "a core of grey charcoal-flecked rubble and . . . an external facing of large squared blocks."[50] It was built up against an existing building, which went on being occupied. Outside the wall there seemed to have been "a contemporary defensive ditch not less than 18 m. wide," whose "exact stratigraphical relationship" to the wall had been destroyed. By the early sixth century, however, "the presumed ditch had silted or been filled up and was being used for the dumping of rubbish, mainly pottery. There then followed the cutting of a second ditch . . . and, nearer to the wall, the deposition of successive rough metallings above the horizontally truncated fill of the first presumed ditch." This suggested that a period of neglect was followed by "a revival of defensive activity," probably to be associated with Belisarius, who, according to Procopius, had the wall repaired and a defensive ditch dug outside it after capturing the city in 533.

The rest of the sixth century was another period of inactivity, represented by windblown and water-formed deposits, followed by "a change of use . . . with a metalled and rutted road being laid in the area adjacent to the wall." This road was at least 11 meters wide with three main surfaces, all of them rutted by wheeled traffic, and "the ruts appeared to veer from the alignment of the wall south-eastwards, suggesting that there was an obstacle, such as a tower projecting from the wall just east of the excavation." Above the silted ditch was constructed a building with at least five main structural phases. Both road and building date from the beginning of the seventh century, if not later, and it was not clear how long they went on. On top of the latest surface of the road, however, adjacent to the wall, building materials were found suggesting a repair of the wall, which will have been well into the seventh century or later and which may be associated with the Arab invasion at the very end of the century.

Some of these phases can be related to findings on the Canadian site. Hurst himself, before our excavations were even planned, discussed the presumed line of the wall along the Teurf el-Sour and put forward three hypotheses, all of which we have now confirmed (the comments in brackets are my own).

> An excavation on Teurf el-Sour in 1923 failed to produce evidence of the Theodosian wall. Instead there was a "wall" 5 m. thick, built of hard-packed earth divided into layers 40 cm. thick by thin courses of clay and ash. The excavations identified this with the earthen ramparts erected by Mohriz-ben-Ziyad in the eleventh century, but much of the area is still exposed to view and a more convincing interpretation is that this is simply part of a conventional stratigraphic accumulation, perhaps of successive road or street levels. [Quite right, it is.] A small fragment of east-west wall at the foot of the scarp made by these levels was of grey charcoal-flecked mortar masonry, 2.1 m. wide, with a rough northern face. On superficial comparison the mortar is very similar to that used for the wall on the Salammbo main road site and the width of the mortar rubble construction matches the width of the rubble core at Salammbo. It can be suggested that this was the city wall and that the scarp was created by the accumulation of levels just inside the wall. [Again, quite right.] The wall would not be visible elsewhere in this area because it has been more severely robbed, but it is to be looked for at the foot of the scarp. [We looked and found it.][51]

We began digging in the Teurf el-Sour area in 1976 and continued in 1978 on a site chosen at a point where two streets of the theoretical street grid of the Augustan colony, *decumanus* VI north and *cardo* III east, intersect each other on the very edge of the escarpment (see fig. 3–1). As we have already seen, this was commonly supposed to mark the line of the wall, and *decumanus* VI was moreover the theoretical *decumanus ultimus*, the last street of the city to the north, according to Saumagne's generally accepted reconstruction.[52] We have backed up our excavations on this main site (see fig. 3–1, 2CC1 and 2CC2) with a survey of visible remains and a number of trial trenches further east along the Teurf el-Sour (2CC4, 2CC7).[53]

On the main site, we have verified the existence of *decumanus* VI and *cardo* III, and found the remains of the wall, badly robbed, at the foot of the slope (fig. 4–2). Just as the wall on the British site was built up against an existing structure, so we found that between *cardo* III and *cardo* II it had for some distance been built up against the outer wall of the houses fronting onto the south side of *decumanus* VI, in such a way as to obliterate most of the street (figs. 4–3, 4–4, 4–5).[54] This street, as it existed when the wall was built in the 420s, was paved down the center, with a surface of beaten earth at each side, and had a fine vaulted stone drain 1.5 meters high beneath it, with an underground conduit, probably for fresh water, running alongside the drain. When the wall was built, the vault of the drain was removed, and the drain filled in with stones set in mortar to serve as a foundation for the facing blocks of the wall. But the wall turned northeastward, away from the line of the *decumanus,* some few meters short of the intersection with *cardo* III, and the short stretch of the *decumanus* left west of *cardo* III, which now had no function, save to give access to the wall, rapidly became a garbage dump, very rich in organic matter, pottery, and coins (fig. 4–3).[55]

Decumanus VI in this block was climbing a hill, rising from 2CC2 near *cardo* II where the street level in the 420s was clearly not much higher than the present ground level in the fields to the north, up to the level of the plateau beyond *cardo* III, which, as we shall see, we now know to be man-made. The incline on the street is built up of a red clay packing which fills the space between the vaulted drain on the north and the deep-set foundations of the house in the corner of *decumanus* VI and *cardo* III to the south (house 1). Although the wall had been heavily robbed at this point we could see where it had been, because the characteristic gray mortar belonging to the core of the wall, such as we have already met on the British site, still adheres to the surfaces to which it had originally been bonded and stands out vividly against the red clay packing beneath the street, at the point where this is revealed by the cut which the wall itself made across it. The same gray mortar also reveals the line of the wall across the corner of a structure of unknown purpose and dimensions, which we found below the robber trench north of the *decumanus,* and had been used for the stone packing of the filled-in drain, contrasting strongly in color with the yellowish sandy mortar originally used to build the drain.

As already referred to, the facing blocks of the wall rested on the filled-in drain, and two such blocks were found in situ, while other blocks now robbed could be traced by the impression which they had left in the mortar. The facing block found in 2CC1 appears to have formed part of the actual outer face of the wall, in which case the wall at this point will have been 3.5 meters wide, as in the British excavations (fig. 4–4). There is, however, some evidence to suggest that there were three rows of facing blocks, and the only other block that we found, in 2CC2, may not belong to the outer row. In any case, not only are the two blocks on different alignments, but the face of the wall, as defined by the impressions of the blocks in the mortar above the drain in 2CC1, is not parallel with the outer wall of the two houses fronting on the *decumanus*, against which the rear edge of the wall abutted. Moreover, house 2 (in 2CC2, at the corner of *cardo* II) projects roughly 1 meter further into the *decumanus*, and hence into the wall that replaces it, than does house 1 (fig. 4–5). It therefore seems as if the width of the wall was affected by existing structures. The houses, we may note, continued to be occupied after the wall was built; house 2 in particular shows signs of intensive occupation throughout the fifth century. The building behind the wall on the British site, we may remember, also went on being occupied after the wall was built. Access to the rear of the wall at this period was presumably confined to certain points only.

Most of the core of the wall, like the facing blocks, has been robbed. But parts of it were found in situ in both 2CC1 and 2CC2 and, in the latter, actually lying on the remains of the core, 1.35 meters below present ground level and covered by the fill of the robber trench, there came to light a rotten canvas bag containing a badly deteriorated wad of newspaper and a stock of over 200 dynamite fuses. The wad of newspaper was very hard to separate and read, requiring techniques that the classical archaeologist normally reserves for papyri. One fragment proved to come from a British newspaper and referred to a protest by Crowley (Sussex) parish council to Lord Leathers, minister of War Transport, over preferential treatment accorded to Italian prisoners of war, who apparently were given a ride to work, while British workmen had to walk or bicycle. Lord Leathers was minister of War Transport from May, 1941, to August, 1945, and the bag can hardly have been deposited here before the British capture of Tunis on May 7, 1943. It would seem that, if the fuses were being used on the wall where they were found, this was still being robbed in 1943 or later.

We also investigated the wall further east. Between the lines of *cardines* V and VI, Dr. Wightman undertook a trial excavation (see fig. 3–1, 2CC4) at the point where there remains the upstanding portion of the core of the wall, already referred to by Hurst. At the western end of this upstanding portion, abutting on its rear face, is a cistern whose northern face was the wall itself. The wall in front of the cistern no longer survives above ground, but excavation showed that it continued in the same straight line as in the upstanding part, contrary to what is shown on the standard topographical map of the area (scale 1:2,000), which wrongly indicates that the wall curves outward at this point. This is undoubtedly a misinterpretation of a shadow on the aerial photograph from which this portion of the map was drawn. Given the curve of the escarpment, as one goes west from the cistern, the wall ought to turn southward, but proved to have been so deeply robbed that no attempt was made to follow it further.

Between this point and our main site, however, several patches of stone with the characteristic gray wall mortar are actually visible in the surface of the path that runs along the bank. Several of these were investigated, and two short stretches of wall were uncovered (see fig. 3–1, 2CC7), one on either side of another bend in the bank, near where the line of *cardo* IV meets it. From *cardo* V to *cardo* IV, the wall in fact runs almost at right angles to the orientation of the *cardines*. Between *cardo* IV and *cardo* III, however, there must have been minor changes of direction. Along both these stretches, as also on the upstanding section between *cardo* V and *cardo* VI, the inside face of the wall, which was comparatively rough, was preserved, while the outer face has been wholly robbed.

Between *cardo* III and *cardo* IV, the general line of the wall, if one ignores minor variations, is parallel to that of the rural cadastration, as is the Damous el-Karita and the road alongside it. There is a low field bank on the same orientation between the Damous el-Karita and our escarpment, whose line, if prolonged, runs just inside the wall from *cardo* IV to *cardo* III. It looks as if the rural cadastration here began just outside *decumanus* VI, and that this determined the development of this *insula* north of the *decumanus*, and hence the line of the wall.

Our work this past year did not extend east of *cardo* VI. But it is clear that further east, beyond the line of *cardo* IX, the wall turns sharply northward, before veering eastward again to cross the line of the railway near Présidence station, heading for Bordj Djedid, where it can no longer be followed under the modern development (see fig. 3–1). The line of the wall here is obviously determined by the desire to include within the fortifications the ribbon development along the coast, discussed by Dr. Wightman in chapter 3.

Even though the line of the wall was determined by the extent of the built-up area, it was not everywhere constructed against existing structures, as it was on the British site and on our own main site. A trench across the upstanding section of the wall (see fig. 3–1, 2CC4), cutting back the collapsed edge of an old trench dug by Poinssot and Lantier in 1923,[56] revealed undisturbed levels and showed that there was no structure prior to the wall immediately behind it, although the ground level inside the wall had been considerably raised at the time of construction, presumably because there were structures at this higher level somewhere in the vicinity. The wall had either been built freestanding from the foundation upward, or in an unusually wide foundation trench. Red clay had been packed against the foundations on the outside, and a line of the same red clay marked the new ground level inside, which was 3.25 meters higher than the new exterior ground level (see fig. 3–3). The wall had presumably been faced with ashlar blocks, as on the main site, and, once again, these had been robbed out to foundation level over a width of 1.5 meters, the original overall width of the foundations being 3.5 meters, as on the British site (fig. 4–6).

It was Poinssot and Lantier who claimed to have discovered the medieval earth rampart already referred to above. But our excavations showed that, as Hurst had already guessed, this was nothing more than two layers of compacted surface, found here and elsewhere along the bank, where they have been revealed by erosion and weathering. They probably represent two successive periods of an *intervallum* road along the back of the wall, and pottery recovered from beneath the surfaces in 2CC4 and 2CC7 would be consistent with a sixth-century date for the lower surface, perhaps connected with the repairs of Count Belisarius in the 530s, and a seventh-century date for the later one. The two periods could possibly correspond to the two periods of renewed activity detected by the British team on their site. On the other hand, two similar surfaces were found on top of seventh-century fill on the main site in 2CC2, and the upper one of these appeared to be possibly Islamic; but we cannot say whether they were part of the same *intervallum* road, or perhaps, as we originally supposed, belonged to a building. The British site also showed evidence of new building immediately behind the wall in the seventh century. It seems likely that in 2CC2 we have the same phenomenon, with the same uncertainty whether to date it to before or after the Arab conquest.

It is clear from our excavations along the Teurf el-Sour that the bank and the plateau south of it are, in their present form, man-made. This is not surprising. Excavations for the foundations of the theater and odeon on the southern slope of our hill, not to mention other public buildings and of course the numerous cisterns that are so prominent a feature of domestic architecture at Carthage, will have produced quantities of soil, which must have been dumped somewhere. The Italian excavations have shown that the northwestern sector of the city was not built up before the second century, and, although we do not yet have comparable data for our own sector east of the *cardo maximus*, irregularities in the street grid would suggest that here too development does not go back to the original days of the colony. The bank in its present form has been created by erosion and slippage after the wall that ran along its foot was robbed. The line of the wall was in general itself determined by the limit of the built-up area to be defended; but its precise relationship to existing structures and the question of access at different periods of the wall's existence requires further clarification.

Apart from establishing the line of the rest of the wall, the main problem still to be resolved is that of the towers and bastions. One tower belonging to the wall was destroyed many years ago, near La Malga:

> dans un terrain appelé Ard-Souiria, près du coude que forme l'aqueduc de Zaghouan pour gagner les citernes... une tour circulaire ou au moins demi-circulaire dont le mur construit avec des matériaux de toute sorte noyés dans un mortier composé de cendres, de charbon et de coquillages brulés, mesurait lm.80 d'épaisseur.[57]

The British note the likely presence of a tower in their sector. One of our primary objectives in 1979 will be to investigate the possible presence of towers or bastions along our own stretch of the wall. The contour of the slope of the Teurf el-Sour seems to suggest that they may have existed at each external angle of the wall. This would not be surprising. This pattern is spectacularly illustrated at Kairouan, where the Arab walls presumably go back to a late Roman or Byzantine model. Vegetius, moreover, writing about a generation before the Theodosian Wall was built, recommends that straight walls should be avoided; he prefers fortifications "sinuosis anfractibus," and suggests "crebriores turres in ipsis angulis."[58] Grenier, commenting on this text, summarizes the evidence from Gaul as follows: "On constate, en effet, que les angles des enceintes sont, presque sans exception, marqués par une tour, généralement ronde et d'assez fort diamètre, le plus souvent 10 mètres, dont le centre se trouve à l'intersection de deux côtés adjacents du mur."[59] The towers need not in fact be round. Von Petrikovits has amply demonstrated that late Roman military architects were nothing if not eclectic.[60] And although towers should normally be within 30 meters of one another, as is the case at most Gaulish sites listed by Grenier,[61] there are notable exceptions. At Trier, for instance,

> towers occur at quite long intervals, being sometimes about 75, sometimes 115 m. apart. It is possible that along the river bank, where few are known for certain, the intervals are even wider. They are round, but not solid, and they project rather further to the inside than the outside. The outer diameter is some 10 m., the inner about 5. Not all of them are known, but there is a tendency for them to occur opposite the ends of streets, perhaps for ease of access.[62]

Trier's walls are of course much earlier than the Theodosian Wall (no later than 353, and almost certainly a century earlier), but the parallels may be suggestive.

Finally, it should be pointed out that the towers will have served as platforms for catapults, although we do not know how much artillery Carthage may have had. Todd has recently pointed out what a shortage there was of artillery in the fourth century, concluding that "it is . . . unlikely that *ballistarii* were stationed as a matter of course in cities, even in cities as important as Rome."[63] The same will no doubt have been true for Carthage.

So much work to fortify the city after so many years, and to so little purpose: the wall was built, but the Vandals still walked in, perhaps through treachery. In the deposit of garbage which accumulated on the surface of the *decumanus* VI behind the wall right after it was built, there are notable quantities of lamps, sherds of amphoras which had originally brought wine from the East to Carthage, and oysters. It suggests a picture of the defenders sitting up at night waiting for the Vandals, assuaging their fears with wine and oysters.

NOTES

1. Cf. Polybius 1. 73, 75; cf. A. Audollent, *Carthage romaine* (Paris, 1901), p. 143: "Les alluvions de la Medjerda (Bagradas), en modifiant peu à peu tout le littoral, ont rattaché la presqu'île d'une façon plus solide à la terre ferme; elle n'apparaît, à l'heure actuelle, que comme une sorte d'éperon." Cf. also H. H. Scullard, *Scipio Africanus: Soldier and Politician* (London, 1970), pp. 116–17, with map showing approximate ancient coastline, p. 161. (Fig. 4–1 shows the modern coastline.)

    2. Strabo 17. 3.

    3. Livy epit. 51; Oros. 6. 22. 5.

4. Malcolm Todd, *The Walls of Rome* (London, 1978), pp. 22–45.

5. Appian *Punica* 95. 127.

6. Ibid., 80.

7. M. Sznycer in *Rome et la conquête du monde méditerranéen*, ed. C. Nicolet, vol. 2, *Genèse d'un empire* (Paris, 1978), pp. 555–56.

8. A. W. Lawrence, *Greek Architecture*, 2d ed. (Harmondsworth, 1967), pp. 230, 235.

9. R. Duval, "L'enceinte de Carthage," *CRAI*, 1950, pp. 53–59. Cf. Pierre Cintas, *Manuel d'archéologie punique* 2 (Paris, 1976), pp. 127–31, also somewhat sceptical.

10. F. Reynier, "Remarques sur la topographie de Carthage à l'époque de la troisième guerre punique," *Mélanges Piganiol* (Paris, 1966), pp. 1,281–90.

11. G. G. Lapeyre, "L'enceinte punique de Byrsa d'après les dernières fouilles de la colline Saint-Louis de Carthage," *RAfr* 360 (1934): 336–53; S. Lancel, J. Deneauve, J.-M. Carrié, "Fouilles françaises à Carthage (1974–1975)," *AntAfr* 11 (1977): 20–21, 32, 65, 67, 73–76.

12. On the *fossa regia*, see esp. L. Teutsch, *Das Städtewesen in Nordafrika in der Zeit von C. Gracchus bis zum Tode des Kaisers Augustus* (Berlin, 1962), p. 10 n.32; R. M. Haywood, "Roman Africa," in *An Economic Survey of Ancient Rome*, vol. 4, ed. Tenney Frank (Baltimore, 1938), pp. 3–4 (with references to earlier discussions and to epigraphic evidence).

13. Cf. P. Romanelli, *Storia delle province romane dell' Africa* (Rome, 1959), p. 44.

14. On the development of Roman frontier policy, see Edward N. Luttwak, *The Grand Strategy of the Roman Empire from the First Century A.D. to the Third* (Baltimore and London, 1976), brilliant but flawed, cf. reviews by E. M. Wightman, *Phoenix* 32 (1978): 174–79; by myself, *AJP* 99 (1978): 527–29; and others.

15. J. Desanges in *Rome et la conquête*, ed. C. Nicolet, vol. 2, p. 627.

16. These campaigns and those that ensued against Tacfarinas have generated an enormous literature; discussion and further references in Romanelli, *Storia della province romane dell' Africa*, pp. 175–86; Marguerite Rachet, *Rome et les Berbères* (Brussels, 1970), pp. 58–126; Marcel Benabou, *La résistance africaine à la romanisation* (Paris, 1975), pp. 57–84.

17. Suetonius *Aug.* 48.

18. F. de Pachtère, "Les camps de la IIIe légion Auguste au premier siècle de l'Empire," *CRAI*, 1916, pp. 273–84.

19. *CIL*, 8. 10018, 10023.

20. Rachet, *Rome et les Berbères*, pp. 79–80.

21. Cf. François Baratte and Noël Duval, *Haïdra: les ruines d' Ammaedara* (Tunis, 1974), pp. 11, 26, 58.

22. Tac. *Ann.* 3. 74.

23. So de Pachtère; at least Cethegus was not proconsul before this, but he

may in fact have been proconsul ten years later, after L. Calpurnius Piso, cf. *Der kleine Pauly* 1, col. 1119; *PIR²*, C1336.

24. Tac. *Ann.* 3. 21; Helvius Rufus won the *corona civica*, took Civica as an additional *cognomen*, rose to be *primus pilus*, and retired rich enough to donate public baths to the town he retired to, *CIL*, 14. 3472.

25. C. M. Wells, *The German Policy of Augustus* (Oxford, 1972), esp. pp. 99–100.

26. S. von Schnurbein, *Die römischen Militäranlagen bei Haltern* (Munster, 1974), argues that there was not room for a whole legion in this key base, and he may be right, at least in the last phase, when part of the base is perhaps made over to nonmilitary uses, but cf. my review in *Britannia* 8 (1977): 463–66.

27. S. S. Frere and J. K. St. Joseph, "The Roman Fortress at Longthorpe," *Britannia* 5 (1974): 1–129; on so-called vexillation fortresses, pp. 6–7.

28. Wells, *The German Policy of Augustus*, p. 8; cf. Florus 2. 29.

29. Tac. *Hist.* 4. 48. The responsibilities of the proconsul and the legionary legate were not clearly defined ("mixtis utriusque mandatis"), a source of trouble later.

30. Michael P. Speidel, *Guards of the Roman Empire* (Bonn, 1978), pp. 19–22.

31. *CIL*, 8. 18042, "cohors abest quae omnibus annis per vices in officium proconsulis mittitur," cf. R. Cagnat, *L'armée romaine d'Afrique et l'occupation militaire de l'Afrique sous les empereurs* (Paris, 1913), pp. 211–15.

32. "Lettre de M. Gauckler à M. Cagnat...", *CRAI*, 1904, pp. 695–703; on the natural strength of the position, p. 702: "Nul emplacement ne pouvait mieux convenir à un poste militaire.... Les avantages stratégiques de ce point élevé sont tels qu'il a de tout temps constitué le centre de la défense de Carthage." Cf. A. Audollent, *Carthage romaine*, pp. 246–49, with addendum p. 843; on the evidence for troops at Carthage in general, idem, pp. 351–57. Colette Picard, *Carthage* (Paris, 1951), p. 62, exhales a breath of scepticism, however.

33. *Chronica Gallica*, ed. T. Mommsen, *Chronica Minora* 1 (Berlin, 1892), p. 658, but with ancestral fear as the alleged reason for absence of walls before this. That Carthage still had no wall in 417 seems to follow from Orosius 5. 1. 5, cf. Audollent, *Carthage romaine*, p. 90; that is, if Orosius is not simply being rhetorical.

34. F. M. Clover in *Excavations at Carthage Conducted by the University of Michigan, 1976*, vol. 4, ed. J. H. Humphrey, (Ann Arbor, 1978), p. 9.

35. Audollent, *Carthage romaine*, p. 90 n.4.

36. *Cod. Theod.* 9. 40. 24, cf. Clover, *Excavations at Carthage 1976*, p. 13.

37. So A. H. M. Jones, *The Later Roman Empire 284–602* 1 (Oxford and Norman, 1964), p. 190, rejecting the allegation that Boniface actually invited the Vandals into Africa; but the evidence that Sigisvult in fact took the city is not conclusive, cf. J. L. M. de Lepper, *De rebus gestis Bonifatii, comitis Africae et magistri militum* (Tilburg, Breda, 1941), pp. 57–63, on the two expeditions.

38. Henry Hurst, "Excavations at Carthage 1976: Third Interim Report," *AntJ* 57 (1977): 255.

39. Quoted by Audollent, *Carthage romaine,* pp. 155–56.

40. Ibid., pp. 154–60.

41. C. Picard, *Carthage.*

42. Cited by Audollent, *Carthage romaine,* pp. 797, 802, 798 respectively.

43. Henry Hurst, "Excavations at Carthage 1974: First Interim Report," *AntJ* 55 (1975): 37.

44. Proc. *bell. Vand.* 1. 21, St. Aug. *Conf.* 5. 8. 15.

45. Audollent, *Carthage romaine,* pp. 224–25.

46. J. H. Humphrey and J. W. Eadie in *Excavations at Carthage Conducted by the University of Michigan, 1976,* vol. 3, ed. J. H. Humphrey (Ann Arbor, 1977), pp. 14–15, 17–18.

47. Andrzej Iciek et al., *Carthage: Cirque-Colline dite de Junon-Douar Chott* (Warsaw, 1974), pp. 45, 121–22.

48. *CEDAC Bulletin* 1 (September 1978), pp. 16–17.

49. Hurst, "Excavations at Carthage 1974," pp. 36–38. It should be added that the position of early cemeteries suggests that there was, as one would expect, a gate by La Malga on the *decumanus maximus,* cf. Audollent, *Carthage romaine,* p. 159. There is a further reference to a possible length of wall in the same work, p. 274.

50. Hurst, "Excavations at Carthage 1974," p. 36. The final interim report on this site, on which what follows is based, is in Hurst, "Excavations at Carthage 1976," pp. 255–60, with interpretative section, p. 255, fig. 9.

51. Hurst, "Excavations at Carthage 1974," p. 37.

52. C. Saumagne, "Colonia Iulia Karthago," *BAC,* 1924, pp. 131–40. On our map (see fig. 3–1), however, for clarity's sake, we have shown the theoretical grid extending beyond *decumanus* VI to the edge of the escarpment.

53. Reports to date by C. M. Wells, "Carthage 1976: la muraille théodosienne," *EMC/CNV* 21 (1977): 15–23; idem, "Carthage, Site 2: The Theodosian Wall," *EMC/CNV* 22 (1978): 9–12 (with appendices by L. Neuru and R. Blockley on pottery and coins respectively); idem, "Canadian Excavations at Carthage, Site 2: The Theodosian Wall," *Current Anthropology* 19 (1978): 390; C. M. Wells and E. M. Wightman, "Carthage 1978: la muraille théodosienne," *EMC/CNV* 23 (1979): 15–18 idem., "Canadian Excavations at Carthage, 1976 and 1978: The Theodosian Wall, Northern Sector," *JFA* 7 (1980): 43–63.

54. *Cardo* III, on the other hand, south of *decumanus* VI, continued in use until well into the seventh century or later. We do not yet know whether it ever extended north of *decumanus* VI.

55. An interim report on the pottery by Lucinda Neuru is forthcoming in *AntAfr.*

56. L. Poinssot and R. Lantier, "Notes de topographie carthaginoise: une enceinte de Carthage," *CRAI,* 1923, pp. 306–11.

57. References in Audollent, *Carthage romaine,* p. 183; Hurst, "Excavations at Carthage 1974," p. 38.

58. Veg. *inst. re mil.* 4. 2, written probably in the 380s, see T. D. Barnes, *Phoenix* 33 (1979): 254–57.

59. A. Grenier, *Manuel d'archéologie gallo-romaine* 1 (Paris, 1931), p. 525.

60. H. von Petrikovits, "Fortifications in the Northwestern Roman Empire from the Third to the Fifth Centuries A.D.," *JRS* 61 (1971): 178–218.

61. Grenier, *Manuel*, 1: 403–591.

62. E. M. Wightman, *Roman Trier and the Treveri* (London, 1970), pp. 93, 96–98.

63. Todd, *The Walls of Rome*, p. 82; on our knowledge of such artillery, D. Baatz, "Recent Finds of Ancient Artillery," *Britannia* 9 (1978): 1–17.

V. Geometric Rhythms of the Circular Monument in Carthage

Pierre Senay and Marc Beauregard

As part of the International UNESCO "Save Carthage" project, the Canadian Archaeological Mission I completed three excavation and study seasons on the site of the Circular Monument (fig. 5-1). The preliminary reports[1] of the 1976 and 1978 seasons give a good idea of how far work has progressed and present, among other things, a historical account of the research on the site, a full documentation on the subsisting structures, and a stratigraphical interpretation of the site. The state of the question has been quite enriched from it, and some answers have been provided, dealing with the plan and date of the building.

Among the studies undertaken, there is one that appears to be most informative on the quality of the architectural program of the monument, besides being rather "amusing." It is the study of the geometric rhythms of the monument; that is, the attempt to rediscover the harmonic lines of its composition. This investigation can help not only for the pursuit of excavations but also may yield a clue as to the meaning and nature of the monument itself.

As we know, the Circular Monument stands in centuria B of the map of Augustan Carthage, as drawn by Charles Saumagne, between *cardines* II and III and just south of *decumanus* IV (fig. 5-2). The ruins are made up of two concentric polygonal rings of pillars, completed on the western side by a row of ten pillars forming a facade and indicating the existence of a surrounding square around the two rings. The pillars of the first ring are trapeziform having a curvilinear inner face and a straight outer one. The pillars of the second ring are also trapeziform, though much wider and not as deep. The western facade is essentially a succession of arches; the shape of the facade pillars shows quite clearly that the monument was vaulted, a fact also indicated by the large fragments of collapsed vaulting containing amphorae and scattered all around. Thus it was an important building with a radiating plan that lends itself most naturally to reconstruction of its missing parts. It will be necessary of course in the reconstitution of the harmonic lines to consider as proven the hypothesis of a surrounding square, a hypothesis that appears most probable but that has not yet received its proof (or counterproof, for that matter). The next season of digs may prove or disprove the point.

In the study of the geometric rhythms, the first thing to note is that the length unit used is the "classical" Roman foot of 0.2957 meter; the module selected by the architects appears to have been of 3 feet (0.887 meter), as it is a common submultiple of the radius of both the first and second ring of pillars (fig. 5–3).

To establish the theoretical plan of the building, two axes are drawn, perpendicular to one another; their intersection will be the center of two concentric circles of seven and fourteen modules of radius, namely, 21 and 42 Roman feet. These two circles are divided each into twelve equal segments by tracing four other circles of the same radius, centered on the intersection of the initial circles with the axes. These four circles (eight in all) will cross the initial circles in eight points which together with their centers will define twelve points, dividing thus the circumferences in twelve equal parts. In each of the two initial circles (of 21 and 42 ft.), one can inscribe a regular dodecagon.

By extending either way the sides of the larger dodecagon, fortyeight outer intersections are thus created; they constitute twelve by twelve, the corners of four derived dodecagons. The first and third derived dodecagons have their corners on the extension of the apothems of the initial one; the second and fourth on the extension of the radii. The radii of the derived dodecagons are approximately 24 feet (8 modules), 28 ½ feet (9½ modules), 40½ feet (13½ modules), 78 feet (26 modules).

Centered on the corners of the second derived dodecagon, twelve circles are drawn, touching the corners of the second initial dodecagon (radius of 14 modules or 42 ft.). These circles define the surrounding square, whose sides are the outer tangents to these circles, taken two by two, one on each side of the axis. The square thus determined has a side 130 feet long; that is, 13 by 10.

The inner face of the first ring of pillars is obtained by drawing a circle of the same radius as those that define the outer square, but this time, inside the first dodecagon, centered on the center of the monument. The internal face of the second ring appears when one draws a series of twelve arcs of the same radius as the one that produces the inner face of the first ring; these twelve arcs are centered on the inner intersection of the twelve outer circles which define the square.

The pillars of the first ring are 4 feet wide inside and 6 feet wide outside; the openings between them are 4 feet wide inside and 5 feet wide outside. The internal perimeter is 96 feet or 12 by 8; the outer perimeter is 132 feet or 12 by 11.

The pillars of the second ring are 15 feet wide on the inside and 17 feet on the outside. The openings between them are 5 feet wide inside and 6 feet wide outside. Thus the inner perimeter is 240 feet or 12 by 20; the outer perimeter is 288 feet or 12 by 24. The outer perimeter of the second ring is thus three times the inner perimeter of the first ring.

The facade is made of a series of arches alternately wide and narrow, separated by pillars. The opening of ten that have been cleared are 6 feet and two-thirds wide (for the broad ones) and 4 feet wide (for the narrow ones); the pillars are all 3 feet wide. Unfortunately it has not been possible to link directly those dimensions with internal ones in order to integrate the pattern of the facade with that of the general plan. As the dimensions of the surrounding square are determined by a geometrical formula, it cannot at the same time be part of a simple arithmetic formula. Nevertheless it is possible to set out some of the principles that guided its composition (fig. 5–4).

A first point to underline is the fact that the radiating plan of the building dictates the direction of the passageways leading from the arches of the facade obliquely toward the center; so that in the hypothesis, which we must accept until further discoveries disprove it, of a surrounding square, there is in the outer two-fifths (roughly) of each half-facade, a "blind" zone which cannot be pierced by arches and whose pattern is unknown to us. This "blind" zone is also proved or at least explained by the geometric formula that dictates the division of the rest of the facade, as we shall see.

Another fact to be noted is that there are mathematical coincidences between measures of the facade and measures of the interior. More precisely, the width of the broad arches, 6 feet and two-thirds, is equal to 21 feet (the radius of the initial circle) divided by π; and some of the main points of the facade at 10 feet and one-third and 13 feet and one-third of the axis are the quotient of sixty-five (distance from the center to the facade) divided by two π; and the quotient of forty-two (radius of the second circle) divided by π. Thus the proportions of the inner pattern are found repeated in the articulation of the facade.

If one extends the sides of the surrounding square, at the intersection of this extension with the extension of the radius of the initial dodecagons (at 30° from the axis), one defines thus a point from which the division of the facade in arches and pillars is determined by a simple geometric process. By drawing lines from that point to the main points on the axis and to significant intervals between them, one gets on the half-facade a series of intersections that mark the limits of arches and pillars. The "blind" part of the facade is the area outside the intersection of the facade with the extension of the radius. There are nine points on the axis: (1) the intersection of the axis with the inner circle (defining the inner face of the first ring); (2) the halfway point between no. 1 and the great dodecagon (radius 42 ft.); (3) the halfway point between no. 2 and the great dodecagon; (4) the great dodecagon itself; (5) the one-quarter point between the great dodecagon and the second derived dodecagon; (6) the three-quarters point between the same two; (7) the second derived dodecagon; (8) the halfway point between the second derived dodecagon and the facade; (9) the three-quarters point between the same two. These nine points joined to the intersection of the extension of the side of the surrounding square with the extension of the radius divide the facade in its components, arches, and pillars.

Let us enumerate a certain number of outstanding points; it has been possible to discover the geometric rhythms of the monument in its essential components. The inner pattern is entirely based on two concentric dodecagons, one being the double of the other. The dodecagons, which derive naturally from the larger one, enable us to complete the picture by defining the limits of the surrounding square. The proportions between those various elements determine the proportions of the divisions of the facade.

Some numbers play an important role: seven, whose fundamental function in the ancient numerology is well known, defines the radius of the initial dodecagons (7 and 7 by 2 modules); twelve is, of course, important, as it appears at a simple glance on the plan, as twelve-sided polygons are the major figures; thirteen, playing an important part in the structural composition, is both the number of circles defining the surrounding square and the dimensions of the innermost room and a divider of the facade's length (130 ft.).

A further examination of the details would certainly lead to discovering other connections and other meaningful proportions; it would also be interesting to compare the data we have for the Circular Monument with similar information from other Roman buildings.

When this paper was written for the University of Michigan symposium, only the western facade was known and the circumscribed square was but a working hypothesis. Since then the 1979 excavations have contributed a lot to our knowledge of the plan, as both the northern and eastern facades have been unearthed. It appears now that the two rings of pillars are enclosed, not by a square but by a rectangle. The monument is 38.60 meters in length along the east-west axis, and 31.50 meters in width along the north-south axis, or in Roman feet, 130 by 106. The area thus defined is equal to ten times that of the innermost circle.

The situation of the closer facades is easily explained by the geometric pattern defined before their discovery. The line of the northern facade is the tangent to the circles defining the inner face of the second ring. It has not been possible to have these data put on the plan, but we shall publish soon a study on this subject, a revised paper incorporating all the latest facts. Nevertheless the results of this paper remain sound; they have even been strengthened by the discovery of new facts that fit perfectly the pattern devised beforehand.

NOTES

1. Pierre Senay et al., *Carthage I: rapport préliminaire Carthage 1976*, Cahiers des études anciennes no. 6 (Montreal, 1976).

2. Pierre Senay and Marc Beauregard, *Carthage II: rapport préliminaire Carthage 1978*, Cahiers des études anciennes no. 9 (Montreal, 1978).

VI. A Mosaic Workshop in Carthage around A.D. 400

Katherine M. D. Dunbabin

One of the original objectives of the University of Michigan excavations at Carthage was to discover a sequence of securely dated mosaics that could establish some fixed points in the chronological confusion that besets the dating of mosaics at Carthage. At first sight the results of that aim seem rather disappointing. The House of the Greek Charioteers excavated by the Michigan expedition contained a number of mosaics, the majority definitely dated to its period of construction shortly after A.D. 400, as well as later additions and substitutions. But the condition of most of them was lamentable; they consisted of broken sections of border and even more fragmentary portions of the central fields of the pavements. Nevertheless, these fragments can be linked to a substantial number of other Carthaginian mosaics through the use of several recurring patterns, in which not only the basic elements of the design correspond, but also the manner of rendering certain common details. It is on the basis of such correspondences, due not just to the use of common models, which may be widespread, but to more particular workshop practices, that one can identify individual ateliers. While any single pattern or motif may remain in general use over a considerable period of time, the recurrence of a specific complex of patterns allows for greater precision, and leads to a presumption, where the links are particularly close, that the works containing them must have been executed within no more than two or three decades.

The *triclinium* of the House of the Greek Charioteers contained a mosaic whose central portion was almost entirely destroyed by the *opus sectile* laid over it in the sixth century, but fragments of the border of acanthus scroll were still in place (fig. 6–1).[1] Scroll borders are a common motif at all periods. The individual peculiarities of this one are the continuous leafy branches, smooth on the outside, and with regular spikes tipped with black on the inside; the black-tipped spathes at the point of division of the scrolls and the big three-pointed lily or lotus flowers between them; the pink leaf buds running off from the scrolls; the fruits and flowers on a long stem at their center; the curling tendrils growing between the spikes. Scrolls with some or all of these peculiarities recur on at least five other mosaics from Carthage, either as borders or as elements in the decor. Three of these are mosaics that have already been dated, on stylistic or other grounds, to the late fourth or early fifth century. There seems, therefore, an excellent case for regarding them as a related group.

The closest parallel is the acanthus scroll that forms the upper border of the mosaic of the Offering of the Crane (fig. 6–2).[2] It differs only in that some of the scrolls contain birds instead of fruit or flowers. The mosaic itself contains hunting scenes, arranged on five registers divided by thin, wavy groundlines from which grow small trees and plants. Many of the scenes are fairly stereotyped episodes of the hunt, for which earlier parallels can be established. The fortified villa from which the hunters depart in the top row is, however, a more interesting feature, found on several mosaics dating from the last century of Roman Africa.[3] But the most important feature is the central register, where the six hunters line up frontally on either side of the shrine containing the statues of Apollo and Diana and the crane offered to them in sacrifice. This is not just a conventionally rendered sacrifice as a minor episode, but something more solemn as the central focus of the pavement; the mosaic has been seen, surely correctly, as a monument of the pagan upper-class resistance around the time of the final triumph of Christianity and the banning of pagan sacrifices.[4]

There seem also to be pagan overtones about the second of this group of mosaics with acanthus scrolls, the Mosaic of the Months and Seasons in the British Museum (fig. 6–3).[5] The scrolls here form part of the allover pattern in the field (as well as filling long panels at the sides with more regular figure eights); the lily or lotus flowers, which are here missing from the intersections of the scrolls, appear instead in the border, filling the curls of an undulating ribbon. Enclosed in the scrolls, in addition to the busts of the Seasons in the corners, are panels containing full-length figures of the months; four survive, identified as March, April, July, and November. Of these, April is represented by a figure dancing in front of a shrine, probably a priestess of Venus, and November is certainly a priestess of Isis holding a sistrum; the figures are closely related to the verses and illustrations in the Calendar of 354.[6] Although representations of the Months and Seasons as such are common in Christian art, the choice here of pagan festivals to portray some of the months strongly suggests that the patron himself was a pagan.

Two other mosaics with acanthus scrolls of the same type may be mentioned briefly, since they are of interest less for their own sake than for the links they provide with other designs to be discussed. On one, a border of acanthus scroll runs down one side of a panel containing fish, with a line of nets linked together forming the border on the adjoining side.[7] On the other, scrolls containing birds cover the field of an ornamental mosaic, with pyramids of foliage growing along the diagonals from *craters* in the corners.[8] Finally, another very similar acanthus scroll border occurs on an ornamental mosaic from the Maison de la Course de Chars, which had a sealed coin of Constantius II beneath it, providing a *terminus post quem* of ca. 350–61.[9] The house contained three other mosaics: in the *oecus*, a big, geometric mosaic with stars of guilloche contained in octagons; in the portico in front, a grid pattern of laurel wreaths containing rosettes; and in the center of that, a panel with the circus scene from which the house gets its name. One cannot prove, in the absence of stratigraphic investigations, that all the mosaics in a house were laid at the same time or by the same workshop, and the mosaic with the acanthus border was off in one corner of the house, separate from the rest. Nevertheless, one may note certain recurring ornamental motifs. The flower at the center of the mosaic with the acanthus border appears (alongside many others) on both of the other two ornamental mosaics; the overlapping polychrome bands used to form triangles on the first mosaic are used for lozenges between the stars of guilloche in the *oecus* (they also appear in the House of the Greek Charioteers and in one of the panels attached to the Mosaic of the Months and Seasons);[10] and the border of lotus flowers set back to back also recurs, though not in identical form. None of these elements is unusual in itself; in combination they may allow at least a presumption of contemporary or near-contemporary workmanship, though many of the patterns used would require further study to establish their chronological range. The figured panel in the Maison de la Course de Chars shows the fantastic subject of the chariot race in which, though the setting is the *spina* of the circus, the chariots are drawn by pairs of birds: two pairs survive, the white geese and the green parrots. The subject is known previously on only two mosaics: at Volubilis, in the Maison à la mosaique de Vénus, and on the Small Circus at Piazza Armerina, where the charioteers are children.[11] The House of

the Greek Charioteers also contained a charioteer mosaic, the panel excavated by the Institut National d'Archéologie et d'Art before the start of
the Michigan excavations, and which was shown by the fragment of
border adhering to it to have been placed originally in the middle of the
acanthus scroll at the entrance to the *triclinium*.[12] This showed the four
charioteers of the factions, identified by their names in Greek, standing
within the gates of the *carceres*. The lower part of the panel, with the
horses and chariots, was destroyed, but I think there can be little doubt
that they were driving ordinary teams of horses. Although the use of
much smaller *tesserae* in the figures produces quite a different effect from
those in the Maison de la Course de Chars, some particular points of
similarity in the treatment may be noted: the whip with its curling thong,
for instance, or the head with the hair just showing under the rim of the
round helmet.

Another fragment of mosaic from the House of the Greek
Charioteers that dates from the construction of the house around A.D. 400
was the border of broken maeander from the peristyle; again the whole of
the central field was destroyed.[13] The maeander itself is a common pattern
for borders, and its use probably extended over a substantial period.
Nevertheless, two individual parallels may be useful. It provides another
link with the Maison de la Course de Chars, where it is used around the
small squares in the *oecus* mosaic;[14] and it forms the main border on
another well-known mosaic from Carthage, the peacock mosaic from the
Maison du Paon.[15] Here the peacock stands flanked by roses in the center
of a semicircular area probably intended to mark the setting for a *sigma*-
shaped couch in the *triclinium*. In the angles are scrolls growing from
kantharoi; below, under a band of laurel wreath, are racehorses who eat
the plants that represent the fruits of the seasons—roses, wheat, vines,
and olives—growing from jeweled canisters. These unrelated motifs
have only one thing in common, that they are all associated with concepts of good luck and prosperity: *felicitas*. The motifs are combined, on
this mosaic as on a number of others of the period, with the aim of
evoking such prosperity and probably of ensuring its continuance for the
owners of the house and those who looked at the figures. Nominal Christians might have laid such a pavement, but I suspect that more probably
the patrons here too were pagan. The link with the mosaics of the House
of the Greek Charioteers is less close in this instance: the scrolls in the top
corner, though they have certain similarities to the acanthus border, are
not exactly the same. It could therefore be substantially earlier, perhaps

(to judge from the style) from the middle of the fourth century. Unfortunately, there are few details available of the other mosaics from the Maison du Paon, apart from a fragmentary amphitheater scene from the corridor; only a very rough drawing is given of the ornamental mosaics from the house, which does not permit identification of the patterns used.[16]

The mosaic from the House of the Greek Charioteers for which the largest number of connections can be established is the fish mosaic discovered in 1977 (fig. 6–4).[17] This was again a sadly battered fragment, in which it is just possible to make out the main features: the sea crowded with a variety of fish; a sea monster in the center and the remains of a figure riding it; the head of a Nereid and her legs at the top; a small island at the bottom corner. Mosaics of fish, sea monsters, or fishers are nearly ubiquitous throughout the African provinces at all periods of the Empire, and at first glance there is little distinctive about many of them: normally the sea is represented by a series of short broken lines and closely packed with fish.[18] But in fact the manner of representing the sea varies quite extensively. The lines can be parallel or zigzag, or various combinations of the two; they can be set more or less densely, and on a dark or light background. On our mosaic the sea is represented by a series of close-set parallel straight lines, in which the *tesserae* themselves are set diagonally, in lines of olive green, black, and gray. This is a method that is found elsewhere in Africa, but that is particularly characteristic of a closely related group of Carthaginian mosaics.[19] That these are indeed products of the same workshop as the mosaics of the House of the Greek Charioteers can be confirmed, not only by the very similar method of treating the details of some of the fish, but also by the recurrence of some of the same decorative motifs that have appeared on the group already studied. Thus a panel of acanthus scroll runs down one side of one of these fish mosaics.[20] Another has a lotus-and-ribbon border, similar to that on the Mosaic of the Months and Seasons.[21] A third, less close in its details and with Nilotic plants among the fish, was found in the vicinity of the ornamental mosaic with acanthus scrolls and pyramids of foliage on the diagonals, though it is not certain that it came from the same house.[22]

Although most of this group show only fish or fishers in boats, a more complex scene appears on the mosaic of the Triumph of Venus from the Maison de la Cachette de Statues (fig. 6–5).[23] Here, against the usual background of sea and fish, are set a marine Venus riding in her shell supported by a pair of Tritons, with numerous putti fishing in boats or from islands of rock, and medallions in the corners containing the winds blowing their conches. Not only is the treatment of the sea and the fish the same, but various other details provide a link with the fish mosaic from the House of the Greek Charioteers. Thus the features, particularly those of the Triton on the left, are rendered in a very similar way to those of the head of the Nereid; and the little island in the center, with its towered building and tiled roof, makes it possible to identify the damaged object in the corner of the fish mosaic as a similar island. It may be noted, however, that the border here is a scroll of a type entirely different from the acanthus scroll; evidently the workshop had more than one pattern at its disposal. From the same house came a mosaic of Amazons hunting on horseback, where the lotus-and-ribbon border was used again.[24] The mosaics alone would not necessarily have told us anything about the religious affiliations of the owners of the house. Although the Triumph of Venus had an obvious appeal to pagans, it is a theme that became very popular, both in Africa and elsewhere, in the fourth to fifth centuries. It is occasionally found in contexts that suggest that its religious content could be neutralized to an extent that made it acceptable to at least nominal Christians; for example, on the silver casket of Projecta from the Esquiline Treasure in Rome, where the subject was accompanied by a Christian inscription, which shows that it had been effectively secularized.[25] In the Maison de la Cachette de Statues, however, the pagan loyalties of the owners were proved beyond a doubt by the further discoveries in the house. Underneath the room where the mosaic of Venus was laid, a staircase led down to a large room that had been deliberately walled up. Inside this were found a number of statues and statuettes of pagan deities (Venus, Bacchus, Jupiter, Mithras, Ceres), of votive offerings, and an inscription from the priests of Jupiter Hammon Barbarus Sylvanus to their god.[26] All of these were presumably placed there to be safe from the attacks of fanatical Christians (some were in fact already mutilated), and then hidden by the walling up of the cellar, and the construction of the mosaic of Venus over its entrance. For this method of preservation, one may compare the account from late fifth-century Egypt given by the Christian writer Zachariah of Mitylene of a Christian mob discovering a group of pagan idols that had been concealed behind a hidden door.[27]

Two other fragments of a fish mosaic where the sea is treated in the same way may provide a link with a hunting mosaic whose fragments are in the British Museum (figs. 6–6 and 6–7).[28] Unfortunately details are not preserved, either of the ornamental surround of the hunting scene, or of the circumstances of discovery of the fish mosaic; Hinks says only that it is "perhaps from the same house as the hunting scenes."[29] Clearly this cannot be taken as conclusive proof, either that they are contemporary or that they are from the same workshop. But there are definite similarities between the hunting scenes and those on the Offering of the Crane, in such details as the treatment of the groundlines with the plants growing from them, in some of the animals, and in the fortified house from which the hunters set out. These make it at least an attractive proposition that they are related, and that we have here two further products of our workshop. The Hunting mosaic has been dated variously to the Vandal and the Byzantine period; on the basis of style, I should be inclined to place it a few decades later than the Offering of the Crane or the House of the Greek Charioteers.[30]

Other characteristics of the fish mosaic from the House of the Greek Charioteers lead in a different direction. One feature that is bewildering at first sight is the broken red line that runs down the body of the sea monster beneath the hand of its rider. A similar mannerism occurs several times on the marine mosaics at Piazza Armerina, both in the *frigidarium* and on the mosaic of Arion.[31] The line here can be more clearly recognized as marking the central ridge or fin of the sea monsters' tails. Further parallels can also be seen on the Arion mosaic: the swimming Nereid with her arc of drapery, the twist of the sea dragon's head, its long, pink-striped neck. There are also certain differences in the style: the lines that form the sea at Piazza Armerina, for instance, are not as regular and dense as on the Carthage fish mosaics, and looser zigzags appear among the parallel lines. I suspect that the close-set striations on the later mosaics are a stiffening of the freer earlier treatment. That the Piazza Armerina mosaics in general are so closely linked with those of Carthage that some at least of them must be seen as the work of a Carthage atelier is hardly to be questioned, but most of the parallels that have been noted are with a group of Carthaginian mosaics normally placed at the beginning of the fourth century—the mosaics from the Maison des Chevaux and the Dermech hunting scene in particular.[32] The *sondages* of Carandini and his colleagues are normally now accepted as indicating a date for Piazza Armerina of approximately 310–20 or not long after,[33] but these *sondages* were, of necessity, extremely limited in scope and certainly did not provide dating evidence for all the mosaics. If this early fourth-century date is accepted for the Arion mosaic, it is possible that the workshop that produced it might have maintained its iconography for certain motifs, and some of its individual mannerisms, with only slight changes for nearly a century. But it is also possible that the dating established by the trial excavations should not be applied to all the mosaics of Piazza Armerina. I would tentatively suggest that the Arion mosaic might be placed several decades later, perhaps around the middle of the fourth century; still substantially earlier than our group from Carthage, but closer to them than the conventional dating allows.

The evidence so far assembled brings together a group of mosaics that may be identified, on the basis of the numerous parallels of pattern and of detail, as the products of a single workshop within a limited span of time; but many questions remain unanswered. It is likely that more than one workshop may have been operating in Carthage in the late fourth and early fifth centuries, and it is not at present possible to identify works that might be contemporary but produced by a different atelier. Nor is the relationship clear between our workshop and the mosaics produced in Carthage earlier in the fourth century, for example in the Maison des Chevaux.[34] Another problem concerns the extent to which this workshop also engaged in commissions in other parts of Africa. It is very tempting to identify as its work the Villa mosaics from Tabarka, where around the scenes of the great estate run acanthus scroll borders very similar (though not exactly identical) to those on the Offering of the Crane and the fragments from the House of the Greek Charioteers, accompanied, on two of the panels, by a lotus-and-ribbon inner border.[35] Other examples of similar patterns elsewhere are, however, more debatable.[36] Several of the Carthage mosaics discussed above show a strong pagan tone. This was, however, presumably a characteristic of the patrons rather than of the mosaicists themselves, and one may ask whether the Christians patronized the workshop for the decoration of the basilicas constructed at this period.[37] The most crucial question is perhaps how long the life of the workshop extended; is there continuity into the Byzantine period, or an interruption with the Vandal conquest? Most of the church mosaics of Carthage that are of undoubted sixth-century date show very different characteristics—different patterns, even different materials.[38] On the other hand, there are examples of fish mosaics that look like rather crude versions of our type in the Byzantine level of the Antonine Baths and in the chapel of Asterius, dating to the late sixth to seventh century.[39] If there was continuity, the further question arises of which pavements are to be assigned to the Vandal period, and whether 439 can really be used as a cutoff point for the production of the grander pavements.

NOTES

The text of this paper is given essentially as presented at the conference, with only minor additions and alterations. It is intended as a preliminary study, and many of the conclusions reached are tentative. When the Michigan excavations are complete, I hope to study in more detail the whole group of mosaics found in the excavations in their relationship to other mosaics of Carthage.

1. The mosaics from the first season of excavation in the House of the Greek Charioteers were published in *Excavations at Carthage Conducted by the University of Michigan, 1975*, vol. 1, ed. J. H. Humphrey (Tunis, 1976), pp. 21–46. The acanthus scroll (no. 1) is described on pp. 23–30, pls. 6–11, color pls. la–b; the parallels that follow were pointed out briefly there.

2. P. Gauckler, *InvTun* 607. For the proposal of a date at the end of the fourth or first quarter of the fifth century see I. Lavin, *DOPapers* 17 (1963): 239. The slightly more formalized treatment of the scroll on the Offering of the Crane suggests that the date is even a little later than the House of the Greek Charioteers, and that the early fifth century is therefore indicated.

3. Cf. the villa on the Hunting scenes in the British Museum (see note 28 below). For other examples, see most recently T. Sarnowski, *Les Représentations de villas sur les mosaiques africaines tardives* (Wroclaw, 1978), list on pp. 23–24.

4. G. Ch. Picard, *La Carthage de saint Augustin* (Paris, 1965), pp. 121–24.

5. R. Hinks, *Catalogue of the Greek, Etruscan and Roman Paintings and Mosaics in the British Museum* (London, 1933), 29, pp. 89–96, figs. 98–105, pl. 29.

6. See H. Stern, *Le Calendrier de 354* (Paris, 1953), pp. 205–19.

7. M. Yacoub, *Le Musée du Bardo* (Tunis, 1970), p. 89, inv. 3636; see note 20 below.

8. *Catalogue du Musée Alaoui*, supp. 2 (Paris, 1922), A.337 (*InvTun, supp.* 602a); see note 22 below.

9. R. Hanoune, "Trois Pavements de la Maison de la Course de Chars à Carthage," *MelRome* 81 (1969): 219–56, esp. pp. 240–42, 255, fig. 19.

10. *Michigan, 1975*, vol. 1, p. 24; Hinks, *Catalogue*, 29f, p. 94, fig. 103. For this type of lozenge and its evolution at the site of Djebel Oust, see M. Fendri in *La Mosaique gréco-romaine 1963* (Paris, 1965), pp. 170–71, fig. 19.

11. Hanoune, "Trois Pavements," pp. 242–55, figs. 20–22. Volubilis: R. Thouvenot, "Maisons de Volubilis: le palais dit de Gordien et la Maison à la mosaique de Vénus," *PSAM* 12 (1958): 66–69, pl. 16, 1. Piazza Armerina: G. V. Gentili, *La villa imperiale di Piazza Armerina* (Rome, 1956), 33, p. 38, fig. 25.

12. *Michigan, 1975*, vol. 1, pp. 30–31, pls. 12–13 and color pls. 1d–2. The workmanship in the figures here is much finer than is usual in the mosaics of this date, with the density of *tesserae* per dm^2 ranging between 119–80.

13. *Michigan, 1975*, vol. 1, p. 40, pl. 19c.

14. Hanoune, "Trois Pavements," pp. 227ff., figs. 4–16.

15. A. Merlin and L. Poinssot, "Deux Mosaiques de Tunisie à sujets prophylactiques," *MonPiot* 34 (1934): 129–54.

16. Ibid., fig. 1; for the amphitheater mosaic, see L. Poinssot and P. Quoniam, "Bêtes d'amphithéâtre sur trois mosaïques du Bardo," *Karthago* 3 (1951–52): 144, figs. 7–9.

17. I am currently preparing this mosaic for publication in *Excavations at Carthage Conducted by the University of Michigan, 1977*, vol. 7 (forthcoming).

18. For some examples of different ways of representing the sea, cf. G. Ch. Picard, *RA* 2 (1960): 45–48; J. Lassus, "Vénus marine," *La Mosaique gréco-romaine 1963* (Paris, 1965), pp. 186–88.

19. In addition to the examples cited in the following notes the group includes also Bardo A.7 (*InvTun* 799); and probably also the fragment from the Maison de Bassilica, P. Gauckler, *NouvArch* 15, no. 4 (1907): 431, pls. 25, 26, 1 (*InvTun* 631).

20. Bardo Inv. 3636; see note 7 above.

21. Yacoub, *Le Musée du Bardo*, p. 83, inv. 2807.

22. *Catalogue du Musée Alaoui*, supp. 2, A. 338 (*InvTun*, supp. 602b); the provenance was 70 m south of A.337 (see note 8 above): A. Merlin, *BAC*, 1910, pp. 176–77.

23. *InvTun* 671.

24. *InvTun* 672.

25. W. F. Volbach, *Frühchristliche Kunst* (Munich, 1958), pp. 116–17; for the significance of the theme of the Triumph of Venus, see J. Lassus, "Vénus marine," *La Mosaique gréco-romaine 1963* (Paris, 1965), pp. 175–89, and discussion pp. 189–90.

26. P. Gauckler, *CRAI*, 1899, pp. 156–65.

27. Zachariah of Mitylene, *Vie de Sévère*, 27–35, quoted by W. Kaegi, "The Fifth-Century Twilight of Byzantine Paganism," *Classica et Mediaevalia*, 27 (1966): 251–53.

28. Hinks, *Catalogue*, 58 (fish) and 57 (hunting scenes), pp. 144–48, figs. 161–67, pl. 32.

29. Ibid., p. 148.

30. For the dates proposed see ibid., pp. 147–48 (late fifth or early sixth century); C. Courtois, *Les Vandales et l'Afrique* (Paris, 1955), p. 288 n. 4 (Byzantine); I. Lavin, *DOPapers* 17 (1963): 241 n. 257 (Vandal).

31. Gentili, *Piazza Armerina*, 9, p. 20, fig. 6; and 32, pp. 36–37, fig. 24. The central red ridge on the sea monsters' tails appears also on the big polygonal marine scene from Carthage in the Bardo, inv. 2772 (Yacoub, *Le Musée du Bardo*, p. 83; Lavin, *DOPapers* 17 [1963]: fig. 36). The sea here is rendered by the same close-set parallel lines, but against a blue ground. There are other points of similarity both with the Arion mosaic and with the Carthage group, in the treatment of the sea dragon's striped neck and in some of the fish.

32. e.g., J. Salomonson, *La Mosaique aux chevaux de l'antiquarium de Carthage* (The Hague, 1965), pp. 21, 27; A. Mahjoubi, *CRAI*, 1967, pp. 264–77; for other parallels see Dunbabin, *Mosaics of Roman North Africa* (Oxford, 1978), pp. 197–201 and references there.

33. C. Ampolo, A. Carandini, G. Pucci, "La villa del Casale a Piazza Armerina. Problemi, saggi stratigrafici ed altre ricerche," *MelRomeA* 83 (1971): 141–281, esp. pp. 153–79.

34. The lotus-and-ribbon border is already in use on the peristyle mosaic of the Maison des Chevaux (Salomonson, *La Mosaique aux chevaux*, p. 24 pl. 12, 4); on the other hand, quite a different type of scroll is used as the border of the hunting mosaic (ibid., p. 26, pl. 13). Also very different is the scroll on the hunting mosaic from Dermech (Mahjoubi, *CRAI*, 1967, p. 264).

35. *InvTun* 940; the close resemblance of the scroll here to that on the Offering of the Crane was also stressed by Lavin, *DOPapers* 17 (1963): 239.

36. Thus the relationship between the Carthage mosaics and those of Djemila (cited by Lavin, *DOPapers* 17) needs further investigation, as does that with the tomb mosaics from Kélibia (J. Cintas and N. Duval, *Karthago* 9 (1958): 157–265). There also seem to be a number of parallels with some of the latest mosaics from Thuburbo Maius, suggesting the possibility that a branch of a workshop from Carthage may have worked in the neighboring town at this date. This question should become clearer with the publication of the volume of the *Corpus des Mosaïques de Tunisie* covering Thuburbo Maius.

37. The basilica excavated by the Institut National d'Archéologie et d'Art adjacent to the House of the Greek Charioteers contains a number of the same patterns used in the group of mosaics discussed in this paper. Its publication should cast some light on this question.

38. On the churches of Carthage, see N. Duval, "Études d'architecture chrétienne nord-africaine," *MelRomeA*, 84 (1972): 1072–125, with full references to earlier literature.

39. Antonine Baths: A. Lézine, C. Picard, G. Ch. Picard, *CRAI*, 1956, pp. 425–30 (without a description of the fish mosaic). Chapel of Asterius: N. Duval and A. Lézine, *MelRome* 71 (1959): 342, 351–54, plan 1, pl. 1, 1. A *terminus post quem* is given by three coins of Maurice (582–602).

VII. Vandal and Byzantine Carthage: Some New Archaeological Evidence

John H. Humphrey

It is premature to attempt a historical synthesis of Vandal and Byzantine Carthage. That must await the completion of ongoing studies, including historical chapters on Vandal Carthage by F. M. Clover, on Procopius and Agathias, and on Carthage in the sixth and seventh centuries by Averil Cameron. These chapters are part of the ongoing research in connection with the current Michigan excavations. When the results of all the UNESCO excavations are available five or ten years from now, a great potential for the compilation of several new histories of the city will exist, including one on Byzantine Carthage in preparation by Averil Cameron, to supplement and revise parts of Charles Diehl's great work *L'Afrique Byzantine*.

But all this is to anticipate: at present the archaeologists working in the city can only begin the process by presenting their archaeological evidence for the later history of Carthage. It is premature yet to try to set most of the archaeological information into a firm and detailed historical framework. And one must at all costs avoid the temptation to try to interpret our archaelogical evidence in the light of the historical sources—of being too quick, for example, to associate evidence of disturbance or dislocation in the archaeological record with particular known historical events like the bloody and at least partly destructive fall of Carthage to the Vandals on October 19, 439, or the more peaceful entry of the Byzantine forces in 533, or the final capitulation to the Arabs in 698. At present the two types of evidence are running parallel but rarely overlap or complement each other with great clarity or precision. We possess detailed sequences of occupation for several sites, but rarely can we with confidence link the two types of evidence.[1]

When examining the archaeological evidence for the period A.D. 439–698, it is best to begin with the current archaeological work. Earlier excavators, not least Père A. L. Delattre with his great interest in the Christian buildings and antiquities, worked in this time period, but their reports are bedeviled by a lack of dating evidence and reliable sequences, and they presented few clues as to which century they were dealing with or the nature of the changes that occurred through the Vandal and Byzantine periods. Virtually all our evidence for the economy of later Carthage also comes from the current excavations. There are now published pottery, numismatic, faunal, and paleoethnobotanical reports, supplemented by information on mosaics, inscriptions, and other materials, that shed light on wider economic, cultural, and social questions.

The new archaeological evidence, however, is less rich than we could wish. Although all the teams have perforce to deal with material from the later centuries, the sites now under excavation have not for the most part been chosen specifically because of the light they were expected to shed upon the fifth through seventh centuries. Thus, we need but lack most of the major public buildings, monasteries, quarters for troops, the governor's palace, and so forth, with a detailed record of all the vicissitudes through which they passed during these centuries. Nevertheless, by chance, if not by design, the sites now being examined do present a good range of different kinds of site in use during this period.

During the last four years the Michigan team has been excavating an ecclesiastical complex alongside an early Christian basilica, and part of a late Roman peristyle house (House of the Greek Charioteers) occupied through the Vandal and Byzantine periods. The work of the first three seasons (1975–77) has now been studied, and the picture that is emerging is one of extraordinary complexity. On the basis of our own experience, a few general comments about the problems of archaeology at Carthage may be made by way of introduction.[2]

On an urban site as complicated as Carthage, we have found that the stratigraphic sequence can only be unraveled if equal attention is accorded to every definable and distinguishable layer. There is a natural temptation to equate what was happening at one end of a site with what was happening at the other on the basis of only a superficial resemblance of layers (or loci) or of a rough contemporaneity of dating evidence. But unless the closest attention is paid to the sequence of the stratigraphy, the danger is that layers will be assumed to be contemporary when they are not. This point can be well illustrated from the history of the ecclesiastical complex where we now have evidence for disruption and dislocation at several different dates. At some time in the Vandalic period there was a breakdown in the unified control over and raison d'être for the complex, which was followed by late Vandalic pittings and robbings of *opus Africanum* blocks that followed (or at least resulted in) the collapse of roofs. During the early Byzantine period there was extensive dumping of debris in some rooms. Another presumed roof collapse, followed by the use of certain rooms for rubbish tips, occurred early in the seventh century. A major phase of robbing occurred in the third quarter of the seventh century. More sloping robbings occurred in the last quarter of the seventh century at one end of the complex. Wholesale robbing devastated the site in the Fatimid period (tenth to twelfth centuries). And, finally, additional disturbance occurred in the modern period on more than one occasion. Without a detailed stratigraphic sequence worked out on the basis of and embracing every distinguishable layer or locus, it would have been easy to "concertina" this sequence, to produce only one or two periods of ancient disturbance, since in most instances the disturbances did not apply uniformly to every room in the complex. However, such a compression of events would have resulted in a distortion of the true picture and would have missed the multiform transformations that this and presumably many other sites in the city experienced, transformations often separated only by a relatively short period of time, yet critical if we are to go beyond the broadest generalizations in creating a historical picture. In many cases the dating evidence by itself is not sufficiently precise to permit one such event in the sequence to be readily differentiable from another, with the result that final proof has to rest with the stratigraphic sequence.

This task is not made any easier at Carthage by the nature of the archaeological levels themselves. Because of the systematic stone robbing that all parts of the city suffered at many dates both during antiquity and from antiquity to the present, the stratigraphic sequence may be difficult to reconstruct because one may be left only with "disconnected small islands of stratification" that are "difficult to correlate with each other because of the lack of distinct horizons."[3] There may often be a lack of stratigraphic connections between rooms or between indoor and outdoor surfaces,[4] although with painstaking excavation stratigraphic links can still be established when a number of robbings along the same wall line are differentiated.[5] Another consequence of the archaeological levels is that no one set of physical sections can display the history of a site in its entirety. It is preferable instead to rely upon a series of plans, drawn at each phase or subphase for each area or for each "island of stratification," which can then be superimposed. Physical sections at Carthage are thus of only limited use, "to deal with localized stratigraphic problems or to aid in the examination of individual layers."[6]

Every archaeological site is different and should in the first analysis be treated as an entity unto itself. The days when one could cast one's eye across a city and confidently point to all the events to be associated, let us say, with the reign of Justinian have long since passed. All parts of a city like Carthage are unlikely to have reacted in the same kind of way at the same time. Thus, in the Vandal period private houses often may not have been greatly affected, although public buildings more commonly were. With respect to the churches, the picture is still more complicated, depending upon whether the church in question was Catholic and upon contemporary politics: we might, for example, use as our model the hypothesis that churches passed in and out of use several times during a relatively short period. While the economy of the city as a whole may have suffered during the Vandal period, pockets of the city presumably remained insulated and were not visibly affected. In the Byzantine period, while there may have been some Justinianic revival, the whole city cannot have been rebuilt or redecorated within only twenty-five years. Such reconstruction as may have occurred might have begun with the more important churches and public buildings, although some private houses of wealthier officials might also have been quick to receive treatment; other areas, which ranked lower down the list of priorities, might have remained a shambles for some years. Again, generalizations about the city as a whole based upon insufficient evidence will tend to be misleading. In the seventh century an even more turbulent set of events seems to have befallen the city, ranging from an extraordinary prosperity, in the pattern of the Byzantine cities of Italy and the east, to widespread abandonment and ransacking of public buildings, churches, and private structures. Again, some parts of the city might have seen intensive occupation, while others, abandoned relatively early, became quarries for any who might stand in need of building materials. So many different factors were at work with each plot of real estate, which all need at some point to be brought into account: thus, was the site in question inside or outside the city walls? Were the city walls being maintained or not at that date? Was the site public or private property? Who was responsible for its upkeep—the church, the city, or private owners present or in absentia? Events need not have marched in neat synchronization from one site to the next. Vandal and Byzantine Carthage covered two hundred and sixty years of the life of a major city and the complexity of its history is much greater than one can ever hope to recover. A good way to begin, however, is by building up detailed case histories of a sample of sites, sites that we hope may in one way or another be typical and representative of others in the same class. They can then be combined to produce a picture that gives equal weight to some of the many different things that were happening in different parts of the city at the same moment.

This brings us to the problem of dating the phases on each of the sites to be used in the sample. In most instances, the excavators have not yet published the dating evidence for each of their phases. But even when that dating evidence has been fully studied, problems will remain as a result of the nature of the evidence itself. For this period, we are chiefly dependent upon coin dates. At present the coins still tend to date the pottery rather than vice versa, and in particular to provide the critical *terminus post quem* for a layer or locus. Yet coins will often *not* provide sufficiently precise dating for the rapid sequence of events that the sites witnessed in this period. There are several reasons for this: one is simply that often we do not have enough coins, or enough legible coins, to permit a really close dating. It has been shown that insufficient coins will almost certainly lead to a date that is misleading. A good case in point would be a find of a single coin of Heraclius (610–41). The assumption might be that it suggested a date for the deposition of the layer in question during the first half of the seventh century, perhaps in the second quarter. Yet the level could well date to the very late seventh century or even later. Proof of this comes from coins found in 1976 in the levels of phase III of our ecclesiastical complex.[7] The phase unquestionably fell entirely within the last quarter of the seventh century and perhaps later. Of 120 identifiable coins found, 5 percent belonged to the third and fourth centuries, 76 percent belonged to the fifth or sixth centuries, and only 19 percent belonged to the seventh century. Coins issued in the second half of the seventh century accounted for only 6.66 percent of the total, and only 4 coins dated later than A.D. 659. Yet the phase continued right down to the end of the seventh century at least. The picture was even more misleading for the Fatimid levels (tenth through twelfth centuries) where no coins later than 687–95 were found—over 200 years too early for the *terminus post quem*. For the seventh century, therefore, the coin picture will probably distort the dating conclusions at which archaeologists are likely to arrive. Coins found in isolation or in small numbers are unlikely to provide any precise idea of the date of the level in question. As large a sample of coins as possible is needed in order to arrive at dates that are anywhere close to the truth. If not, suggested dates are always likely to be too early. The problem results from the fact that the Carthage mint seems to have put out a much smaller number of issues under Constantine IV and Justinian II during the second half of the seventh century,[8] being content instead to rely upon the vast numbers of fifth, sixth, and early seventh century coins (including all the Vandalic and Justinianic *nummi*) still in circulation. But dating problems also exist with the Vandal period. For it appears that no bronze *nummi* were minted by the Vandals before A.D. 477 at the earliest.[9] Thus, for the first forty or so years of their rule, Roman coins struck mainly in Rome itself seem to have constituted the small change of the city. Relatively little new coinage evidently reached Carthage during those forty years (and only a very few struck in the east after Carthage had fallen to the Vandals reached the city). It becomes very difficult in fact to date a level securely to the period between, for example, 430 and 490, because, although bronze coinage did begin again with Huneric in 477, the smallest denomination securely attributed to him is four *nummi*; similarly, no single *nummus* can be securely attributed to Gunthamund (484–96), although perhaps some Victory types were struck by him. Secure dating for the later Vandal period is equally problematic, for although Vandalic *nummi* were apparently minted in large quantities for at least the period A.D. 496–533, they remained in circulation well into the seventh century. In other words, a Vandalic level deposited during the first half of Vandal rule is likely to produce no Vandalic *nummi,* but that does not guarantee that the level in question may not have been deposited after the Byzantine reconquest. An additional complication is that some of the Victory type *nummi* possibly were struck under Justinian.[10] And Justinianic *nummi* are also unreliable as a *terminus post quem* because they continued in use for a long time. Again, the size of the sample becomes critical: if the sample is small, it is hard to achieve secure dating. If, on the other hand, the sample is large and only Vandalic coins are present, the level may well date to the late Vandal period. But it is going to be very difficult for excavators to prove that they have indisputably "Vandal levels" on their sites, or to prove that a destruction level or disturbance should be associated directly with the Byzantine capture of the city. The best way to isolate Vandal levels is likely to remain the stratigraphic, whereby levels can be sandwiched between those of the late fourth or early fifth centuries (readily datable, now, thanks to pottery as well as coins) and those of the early to mid-sixth century (also readily datable thanks to the proliferation of Justinianic coins and more easily recognizable pottery).

A final question pertinent to chronology concerns the interpretation of major phases of disturbance on our sites.[11] Where there were major robbings (including the robber trenches that removed walls), should the fills of those robbings be closely linked with and thus serve to date the robbing activity itself, or should they rather be associated with the later redeposition of destruction material at a time when cleaning up was being undertaken? The problem becomes acute on the Michigan site where robbings seem to fall into the early sixth century on the basis of the contents of the fills of the robbings, yet stratigraphically the consolidation was not always accomplished before the later sixth century. Thus, after buildings or rooms went out of use they may not have been put back into use very quickly, and when they were, most of the material used to consolidate the site is likely to be redeposited earlier material—as our team has found in the case of several of the fills of cisterns.[12] One conspicuous instance was a cistern below the House of the Greek Charioteers that contained exclusively fifth century pottery dumped into the cistern only in the Byzantine period. At times when large amounts of earlier domestic and other debris were being carted around a site prior to reconstruction, the reliable *terminus post quem* may depend upon only a very small number of sherds or coins from the deposit as a whole. If they are overlooked, or attributed to "contamination," the evidence of the stratigraphic sequence may be at odds with the evidence of the finds.

Our review of the new archaeological evidence for this period may begin with buildings associated with what is assumed to be one of the parish churches of Carthage.[13] What appears to be a series of superimposed churches, lying between *decumani* II and III south and *cardines* IX and X east, was uncovered by the Tunisian Institute in the course of rescue excavations in 1969–71. Scientific study of these buildings is now being undertaken by the institute under Madame Liliane Ennabli. Although the number of buildings and their chronology are not yet finally determined, there is little doubt that the largest of these churches, found only just below the level of the modern field and with well-preserved mosaic pavements, dates to the sixth century. An earlier and narrower building, probably also a church, contains mosaics dated by their style to the early fifth century. The fifth century ecclesiastical complex that has been excavated by the Michigan team was built into an earlier structure, of which a few, but not all, of the walls were reused. Of the ten rooms in the complex excavated, only one—the room at the center of the *insula*—had a mosaic floor; the rest evidently were paved with mortar floors. Some of the smaller rooms at the west end (numbers 2–5) were perhaps storerooms. The street wall at the west end was evidently built encroaching beyond the earliest street wall to have fronted *cardo* IX. In the next phase of the complex (called phase X-2), various resurfacings occurred, always closely associated with the previous floors and lacking the intermediate dense buildup of occupation or the frequent mortar patches that characterized the later phases. This phase (X-2) was probably still ecclesiastical, since it was relatively tidy, but no single and uniform treatment applied to all the rooms and they may not all have been used for the same purposes for which they had originally been designed. This phase marked the last series of major refloorings in the complex before it was turned over to domestic habitation (by the early seventh century). They were the last well laid and firmly bedded floors in the complex except for one or two isolated examples that occurred during the second half of the seventh century.

There followed a breakdown in the unified control and original function of the ecclesiastical complex, marked by pittings and robbings in the later Vandalic period, by which time roofs must have collapsed. The complex may no longer have been under the direct management of the clergy. Possibly some of the damage also occurred immediately after the Byzantine conquest when a decision may have been made by church authorities not to attempt to put the complex back into operation. We now tend to believe that there was no early Byzantine reconstruction of the ecclesiastical complex as such: any sixth century reconstruction was presumably confined to the new basilica and baptistery to the north, while only simple domestic occupation continued in the shell of the complex after late Vandalic times. Consolidation in the sixth century seems to have consisted of Byzantine dumping of Vandalic occupational material into the pittings and disturbances. Several of the rooms (numbers 6–8) seem to have seen a hiatus in their occupation during much of the sixth century. Well-dated debris layers, formed by dumping and filling, were deposited in the reign of Justinian, particularly in the corridor south of the new sixth century baptistery. Some of this dumping was probably associated with the construction of the adjacent baptistery (as was suggested by the discovery among the dump of a group of paint pots, associated with the latest coin of A.D. 541–43). The room facing *cardo* IX remained in use and several attempts were made there to repair flagged surfaces, while in a few other rooms attempts were made to rebuild walls subsequent to the previous phase of robbing. Most of the rooms, however, evidently saw no habitation for most of the rest of the sixth century except for the corridor, which received a mortar floor dated after a coin of 548–65, and perhaps also rooms 5A and 6 at the center of the *insula*.

A revival of interest in the area and raised living standards compared to the sixth century then occurred in the late sixth to early seventh centuries (perhaps particularly under Heraclius, 610–41). Generally the structures, walls, and floors were now of poorer quality than in the original ecclesiastical phase, and the occupants were relatively unconcerned about leaving many traces of their material culture scattered through the rooms in the form of occupational debris and in the composition of the floors themselves. There was continued use and prosperity in the room (number 2) facing *cardo* IX, and a new flagged floor was put down there. It was probably under separate ownership, perhaps as a shop, and its floor was raised to match that of the adjacent street. The next room to the west, formerly taken up with a drain complex, was filled in, used as a rubbish tip (which included many sections of collapsed vaulted roof and was dated later than an early coin of the reign of Heraclius), and then received a new, poorer quality floor above, perhaps to level it off with the adjacent room number 2. Subsequently rooms 2 through 5 assumed a similar character to each other, with poor quality mortar floors, and room 2 no longer formed a separate unit at the west end. Other rooms saw an even and continuous buildup of occupational material leading to our phase X-1, i, also dated later than coins of Heraclius, when all the rooms examined saw intensive occupation with new floors, occasional fitments, hearths, possible pillar bases, and mudbrick and earth surfaces that were frequently patched and had occupational debris above them. In this period all the rooms were brought back into service for domestic purposes and were used to their maximum potential. But throughout this period individual rooms underwent their own developments and the intensity and character of the occupation varied from room to room and from one moment to another; occupational levels occurred in some rooms earlier than in others.

This phase of great activity ended with another phase of robbing (our phase IIa), dated later than a coin of 659–68. The corridor wall and street walls were robbed, pitting occurred in the corridor, and several other walls were robbed and floors pitted, mostly in order to take out good quality cut stone (*opus Africanum* blocks, wellheads, and threshold stones). This was followed by tipping and general debris levels, and then some desiccation of the earlier tips and surfaces. The complex was put back into use shortly afterward (later than a coin of 674–85) when a common level of occupation—a hard mortar surface—was established in the corridor, flagged floors (of reused stones) were put down in other rooms, and doors were restored between various rooms (phase IIb). Many occupational levels built up, of which some exhibited patches of burning, indicative of fires inside the rooms. Both the flags and the wall preserved in a room next to *cardo* X consisted of reused street pavers.

The following phases (our phases III, i through III,iv) all belonged to the last quarter of the seventh century or later, and exhibited exceptionally intensive occupation. In the corridor more mortar patches, resurfacings, and occupational layers were deposited. Elsewhere some of the floors from phase II continued in use, but at the west end of the site various sloping robbings occurred at the start of phase III; the latest of these robbings (in phase III,i) was later than a coin of 686–87. Then followed a remarkable example of late domestic architecture at the east end of the site, exhibiting shallow walls built on the line of the earlier robber trenches, post-pads, and shallow partitions in the rooms (on different alignments in each of the subphases). Mudbrick and mortar floors were added at frequent intervals, and the mudbrick tips from the sloping robbings were resurfaced. Thresholds to the north suggested that this late domestic area, built *after* all the major walls at this east end had been robbed, extended farther north.

Whereas at the west end of the site in the late seventh century occupation continued in the essentially unaltered ecclesiastical complex, at the east the original ecclesiastical room plan had been altered. This was because no ecclesiastical structures had survived that could be used for walls or floors; thus we find earthen floors, wattle partitions, and post-pads, as the occupants fell back on their own resources, providing us with a pure example of the very latest architecture put up in the city. The mortar and earth floors were normally laid moist or semimoist before being allowed to dry out; some were also beaten or compacted. The walls relied upon mudbrick, timber, and wattle. Wattle partitions were frequent. No vaulting tubes were found in these levels, suggesting that the roofs were flat. No Fatimid pottery has been found in these levels, suggesting that they fell close in time to the fall of the city in 698. The next major phase (IV), one of extensive robbing, should be considered Fatimid because of the pottery.

Another ecclesiastical site is represented by the Circular Monument under excavation by the first Canadian team (Pierre Senay) and discussed in chapter 5.[14] Although it is now thought to have been constructed in the second half of the fourth century, its identification and later history concern us here. Its identification has continued to elude scholars although Picard's hypothesis of a Christian connection has become more likely in view of the late date. As a large centralized building (diameter ca. 40m) with a circular and taller (perhaps domed) interior— taller because the foundations for the central circle were much deeper— surrounded by an ambulatory that was also circular, it most closely resembles some of the later fourth or fifth century *memoriae* or *martyria* in the west. (The plan seems to be unique in Roman North Africa.) Attached to its west side there was a straight facade. Piers recorded by Lézine suggested that the same may have been true at the south, but to the north there is no room for an identical facade and enclosing frame since it would have fallen on the far side of the sewer of the *decumanus* IV north (which always seems to have remained in use) and up against the buildings of the next *insula* to the north. Thus, there can have been no frame or facade that was completely symmetrical on all sides, and the main entrance was presumably from the west. The main difficulty in interpreting the building comes from the levels: there were evidently galleries placed below the contemporary ground level in the substructures; on top of those massive foundations would have been the main floor of the building, which would have risen slightly above the contemporary ground level outside. Presumably one had to walk down steps to reach the substructures or up slightly to reach the main floor of the building. To the west, *cardo* II east may have become completely blocked by this date, although there may have remained access along *cardo* III east on the east side.

Perhaps shortly before the Vandal conquest the Circular Monument underwent some alterations—the walling up and masking of some of the arches of the substructures on the western facade, and the raising of the ground level in front of that facade. Then at some date in the fifth century the building seems to have been robbed or damaged and perhaps put to another use; an early Roman cistern below the floor of the substructures, which had been reused when the Circular Monument was first built, was filled in. Much more substantial changes occurred in the Byzantine period. A systematic raising of the ground occurred around the building on the west and inside the galleries of the substructures. The area in front of the west facade was turned into a series of rooms paved with mosaics (some were lifted by Lézine). One of them, about 2.5 meters in width which ran along the north half of the west facade, was paved with an elaborate geometric mosaic of good workmanship (this is dated Byzantine by the excavators, although from a stylistic point of view it may be earlier, dating to the initial construction period of the building: one recalls that a coin of Julian was found below one of the adjacent mosaics by Lézine). At the same time new floors were put down at a much higher level inside the substructures of the monument, bringing them up to the elevation of the mosaic rooms outside. At about this time or shortly after, a basilica (Lézine's basilica) seems to have been built immediately to the west. (Recently evidence for another, earlier basilica below has been found.) It reused some earlier wall lines but its apse at the west end completely encroached and blocked the line of the former street. There is considerable difficulty in identifying and equating the phasing between the Circular Monument and the basilica(s) to the west because of differences in elevation. This was complicated by the fact that there had presumably been a street running below the east end of the basilica and that the structures on the east side of that street had presumably been lower than those to the west, and because when the Circular Monument was built it utilized massive substructures and a basement level that buildings on the other side of the road did not. We would prefer to suppose that the geometric mosaic put down just west of the building was at least contemporary with (if not earlier than) Lézine's adjacent basilica, which was paved with the fine Byzantine mosaic *aux oiseaux* in about the mid-sixth century. The geometric mosaic later went out of use and was covered with a friable mortar floor (not with mosaic); later floors in the basilica substructures (if any existed) have not survived. However, a later phase (or phases) is attested by tombs found in 1976 and 1978 as well as by Lézine, at various elevations at differences of 1.2 meters and more, which were cut through the mosaics and other floors around the basilica, mostly cist graves covered with large reused stone slabs (one found in 1978 contained two children, was oriented east-west, and was dated to the seventh century).

Despite the fact that all the dating evidence is not yet available, what stands out as of particular interest to us is the damage or disuse that the Circular Monument seems to have seen during much of the Vandal period (one may recall that the nearby odeon and theater suffered heavily at the moment of the conquest), followed by renovation and raising of the ground level in the Byzantine period, when a new basilica was built adjacent and some high quality mosaics put down. This may parallel to some degree the evidence from the ecclesiastical complex on the Michigan site, where there was considerable disturbance of ecclesiastical structures during at least some of the Vandal period, followed by reconstruction in the Byzantine presumably directed initially to the church and baptistery. It is becoming clear that the Byzantines attached particular importance to the task of renovating, or putting back into operation, existing churches and in other cases to building new churches. Mosaic workshops were also kept busy during much of the sixth century, particularly in churches.

Activities of considerable complexity are also attested in this general period for an important public area, that of the island of the circular harbor[15] (British excavations under H. Hurst). In the Roman period perhaps from about the late second or early third century, the island served as a monumental complex approached by a causeway, entered by a three-bay monumental arch or gate, and surrounded by a circular wall that had colonnades or arcades inside and outside it. At the center of the island was a temple (temple 2) and an octagonal building the identification of which is uncertain. There is little evidence for other structures within the large circular enclosure, which may have served as an open *platea*. Robbing of these structures seems to have occurred in the Vandal period. The robbing of the temple is given a minimal date of the late fifth century while a destruction deposit overlying the steps west of the octagonal building is dated by finds not earlier than the mid-fifth century. Some tombs have also been dated to the fifth century. Thus it appears that the monumental Roman buildings at the center were finally obliterated by the later fifth century or thereabouts, although they may of course have gone out of use some time before that (as would be likely assuming that the temple was pagan and not converted to Christian use). The excavators have also suggested that there was a time lag between the robbing and the occupation layers and pits that followed, which are dated to the early to mid-sixth century.

Early Byzantine redevelopment of the island and harbor along roughly the same lines occurred on a considerable scale, which implied to the excavators that by the end of the Vandal period the harbor had fallen into a considerable degree of neglect and possible disuse. The wider implications of such a conclusion need to be assessed carefully; the Vandals certainly used harbors at Carthage for their fleet and other vessels, but if the rectangular harbor continued to serve as the main commercial harbor, then perhaps it was unnecessary for the circular harbor to be maintained. Or perhaps alternative harbors were developed, particularly as a result of problems that occurred due to the water level: there seems to have been a pronounced rise (1 m) in sea level between the Roman and Byzantine periods, which may have caused problems for shipping in both harbors.

At any event, systematic work done in the sixth century implied that the Byzantines did intend to put the circular harbor to some use. The level of the island was reduced (thereby removing many of the Roman and Vandal levels) and garbage and earth were dumped over and beyond the Roman quay wall, enlarging the island out to a probable new Byzantine quay wall built six meters beyond the Roman. The tips which covered the former wall included good groups of pottery of the second quarter of the sixth century. Dumping into the water next to the Roman quay might have made it difficult for ships to dock there; the narrower channel which was now created around the island could thus have been dredged more easily.

However, although massive earth moving was undertaken on the island, the purpose of all this activity remains obscure. There seems to be evidence that the monumental entrance and perimeter colonnades were reconstructed in the sixth century, but have monumental Byzantine structures at the center of the island simply disappeared without trace or were none ever erected on the new enlarged island? Perhaps Byzantine plans for the island were never completed. The surviving features that do belong to the Byzantine period hardly give the impression of a monumental center. Near the middle was the small building 4 with walls constructed of stones set in rammed earth. There were also stone and earth surfaces and many earth and gravel occupation levels adjacent. A few other somewhat irregular structures and cisterns reported by Merlin and others presumably also belonged to this general period. Inhumation burials have been found at various places on the island, both close to building 4 and over the Roman quay wall at the north. They were generally aligned east-west. One cist burial cut through the footings of building 4 and so probably postdated it, but the building may have remained in use after some of the burials. These cist burials were normally covered by large stone slabs, like those elsewhere in the city. The robbing of the Roman quay wall at the north preceded three burials of adults in grave pits, all uncoffined and arranged east-west with their heads at the west. One lay directly on the remains of the quay wall, but two others were later stratigraphically. Thus, not all the burials on the island were necessarily contemporary, and one should perhaps beware of assuming that the presence of burials always means a break in the occupation of a site. Also presumably of a late date were the remains of kilns (perhaps for pottery) and associated with them many local amphora sherds including wasters found in rubbish pits nearby. Whether these kilns were sixth or seventh century is not yet established.

In some important respects the later history of the rectangular (commercial) harbor appears to parallel that of the circular.[16] The American excavations of L. E. Stager have shown that a presumed warehouse or storage building was constructed between about A.D. 360 and 380. It stood about 28 meters back from the Roman quay wall and the intervening open area was paved with flags. The building rested on parallel foundation vaults that ran back for at least 22 meters. There is evidence for a break in continuity around the end of the fifth century when at least one garbage pit was cut through the rugged plaster floor and leveling fills of the building. The pitting was subsequently sealed by another plaster floor which may mark a major early Byzantine remodeling and reconstruction of the harborside facilities. A well was inserted in the vaulted foundation to provide water. At the same date or in the late fourth century phase, a colonnade with a rough plaster pavement—the columns or piers faced toward the warehouse, a continuous wall on boulder and mortar footings faced toward the quay wall— was built in front of the flagged area, and the quay wall itself was rebuilt.

The paved area of the quayside and the buildings that went with it continued to be used into the seventh century. At some undefined moment in the seventh century, however, the rectangular harbor ceased to fulfill its earlier function. Kilns were dug into the last two phases of the plastered quays, and waster heaps were tipped over the quay wall and the harbor sediments. One corner of the warehouse was demolished and converted into a burial ground (the top of the vaulted foundation was sheared down to prepare a flat area for the burials) and the well was deliberately filled in. It would be of particular interest to establish the precise moment when the rectangular harbor ceased to function as a harbor. Presumably the harbor became silted up and other docking facilities may have been used during the declining years of the city. Thus the harbor buildings were demolished or robbed, and the open spaces invaded by kilns, now able to benefit from a location very close to the nucleus of the city. The kilns and burials paralleled what was happening on the island of the circular harbor, and both harbors may have fallen into neglect at about the same time. The hint of some abandonment or change in the fortunes of the warehouse in the later fifth century also parallels the disturbances noticed on the island at about that time. The main difference between the two harbors would thus lie in the major phase of reconstruction attested for the commercial harbor in the later fourth century (missing from the island, it appears). It will also be important to know how long the Byzantine work of reconstruction on the island was maintained in good condition. Did the circular harbor go out of use earlier than the rectangular? Is there additional corroborating evidence from the rectangular harbor that it fell into disuse in the Vandal period? And what other harbors may have remained in use throughout the Vandal and Byzantine periods, to house the fleet and provide continuous links with the rest of the Mediterranean?

Another important public construction, the Theodosian city wall, may be thought to act in some ways as a barometer of the health of the city throughout the period under consideration. Yet, as we shall see, defenses in a state of excellent repair and preparedness need not imply order and prosperity throughout the city, nor need the converse always be true. An extremely important sequence for the history of the defenses and adjacent structures has been worked out by the British team under Henry Hurst at their Avenue Bourguiba site at the southern edge of the city.[17] In the Roman period at this southern limit of the built-up area a respectable *opus Africanum* building fronted onto an east-west street that lay south of the original southernmost street of the original Augustan city grid. It was probably a block of small commercial and domestic premises and had a long life.

The sequence of the defenses (the wall itself and other features outside the wall) may be summarized as follows:

1. The city wall was built around 425 with, 2 meters to the south of it, a presumed contemporary defensive ditch no less than 18 meters in total width. Inhumation burials of two children were placed along the south edge of the wall foundations shortly after the construction of the footings; the burials were arranged east-west with their heads at the west and one may have been coffined. Another burial nearby had its head at the east, while a fourth was cut through the fill of the presumed ditch.
2. By the early sixth century the ditch had silted or been filled up and was being used for the dumping of rubbish, mainly pottery.
3. A second ditch, no less than 10 meters in total width, was then cut farther out in front of the wall, while successive rough metalings were placed over the truncated fills of the presumed first ditch. Both the new ditch and metalings were predated by pottery of the early sixth century. These activities marked a revival of defensive activity best associated with Belisarius's known work on the defenses (which included the digging of a ditch outside the wall) following his capture of the city in 533, and following Vandal neglect of the defenses (which is attested by Procopius).

. The first metaling was followed by two more of compacted earth and rubble, the second being placed over a large pit dug into the first surface. At some date the ditch was also recut.

4. A deposit of windblown material 70 centimeters thick and the silting up of the recut ditch, probably contemporary with each other, pointed to a new period of inactivity on the defenses, dated by finds to no later than the end of the sixth century.

5. In the early seventh century at the earliest, the defenses had become obsolescent with a metaled and rutted road no less than 11 meters wide built adjacent to the wall and a building (building 5) placed over the silted-up second ditch. The road received three main surfaces, all exhibiting wheel ruts, while building 5 went through at least five main structural phases.

6. There were hints of later repairs to the wall in the form of building materials found above the topmost road adjacent to the wall. This would presumably have occurred after building 5 had gone out of use, and must date at least well into the seventh century. It has been suggested that it occurred at the time of the Arab attack on the city.

The buildings immediately inside the line of the wall seem to have been directly affected by the history of the defenses. The sequence inside the wall may be summarized as follows:

A. The earlier Roman masonry building (building 1) saw the city wall abutted directly up against its south wall in approximately A.D. 425, but probably the building continued in use for some time thereafter, since its south wall was not removed by the city wall.

B. The end of building 1 was marked by a mass of destruction debris that sloped down from the direction of the wall (was it a deliberate rampart?) and was sealed over by an extensive mortared surface.

C. The area was then used as a rubbish tip for the dumping of organic material, although there may have been some slight occupation inside the wall at the same time.

D. Next the whole area was leveled up extensively by a series of tips all deposited within a short space of time. They presumably represented a deliberate attempt to level the site for building, since directly above them were found the three phases of building 4. Building 4 had a compacted earth makeup skimmed with white plaster for the floor and a simple earth surface to the south. The walls that went with this building must have had very shallow foundations since none were found. In the second phase there was evidence for an east-west wall and three column or pier bases, with surfaces of beaten earth showing traces of mortar. More surfaces were put down in the third phase. A cistern from building 1 was also used with buildings 4 and 2 (see point E) and a presumed water tower or tank was used with building 4.

E. Building 4 was succeeded on roughly the same site by building 2, which was placed on a distinctive deposit of mudbrick debris (the destruction deposit from building 4) which probably served as its makeup. The plan of building 2 is better known than that of its predecessor; it was L-shaped with rooms along the north side and on the west side running up to the back of the city wall. There was probably an entrance through the east side from the yard and cistern area, where the cistern access was rebuilt at this time and a new overflow channel from the cistern was constructed. Building 2 had rough, unmortared limestone footings that were probably sills for walls made of mudbrick. The only surviving floors were of beaten earth, although more substantial metalings existed outside. The standard of living in this structure was clearly inferior to that of the *opus Africanum* building and it gave no hint of ever having received painted wall plaster, mosaics, or architectural embellishments. The finds pointed to a general domestic usage with no indication of specialized activities. A modest standard of living was also suggested by the scarcity of durable food remains. The excavators have suggested that it, like poor dwellings in the area today, was used to house both humans and animals. It passed through three phases, but they need not have occupied many years in view of the insubstantial nature of the structures.

F. The excavators have placed a number of burials in the period following the abandonment of building 2. Two cist burials contained three supine infants aligned east-west (heads at the west); one produced a coin of Heraclius, providing a firm early seventh century *terminus post quem*. A subrectangular pit contained a baby inhumation slightly crouched in an amphora; the baby, in turn, lay over a supine adult placed in two amphoras laid end to end (both burials were again east-west).

G. The last building to occupy this site, building 3, was even more slight than its predecessor. It spread over the area of the former court of building 2, but was placed on a different alignment. Some of the walls of the earlier building were reused as a foundation. It was associated with beaten earth surfaces outside. The *terminus post quem* for this four-roomed structure was again a coin of Heraclius (610–41).

The definitive correlation of what was happening inside the wall with the sequence of the defenses must await the full report. However, we would suggest that, instead of associating the construction of building 4 (see point D) with the new work on the defenses under Belisarius, the presence of structures directly inside the wall is more likely to belong to a period when the defenses were *not* being fully maintained. Thus, it might be best to stretch the life of building 1 well into the fifth century. It finally fell into disuse well into the Vandal period and was then covered over by a mass of debris that was sealed by a mortared surface at the same time that the wall was put back into operation (see points B and 3). The destruction debris served to create a kind of rampart up against the back of the city wall. Only after the defenses had begun to be neglected in the later sixth century was building undertaken again on the inside (see point D). Building 2 (see point E) would have followed in the second quarter of the seventh century or thereabouts, contemporary with building 5 (see point 5). The burials, which would *not* necessarily mark a separate phase and could have overlapped with habitation on the site, would date to roughly the third quarter of the seventh century as could building 3 (see point G), just before the final repairs to the wall (see point 6).

It goes without saying that this location directly inside the late city wall, which at times was not well maintained and the open spaces next to which would have attracted rubbish, must have been one of the least desirable, even for seventh century Carthage. These structures should therefore represent one end of the scale, and they are likely to contrast markedly with contemporary habitations in the center of the city which could make use of more solidly built Roman and Byzantine structures (as in the shell of the ecclesiastical complex).

The sequence from the British Avenue Bourguiba site also serves to shed light on and to complement the evidence from the second Canadian excavation[18] on the more attractive north side of the city, where elaborate houses of the middle to late fourth century, exhibiting good *opus Africanum* construction with intervening mudbrick walls and paved with polychrome and black-and-white mosaics, stood on the edge of a scarp looking north up the coast toward the headlands, enjoying pleasant vistas and cool breezes. The city wall was then built, butting up against the walls of the houses on the south side of *decumanus* VI north between *cardines* II and III east. (A short distance northeast, however, the wall may *not* have been built up against standing buildings.) The wall was placed over the destroyed half of the *decumanus* between *cardines* II and III; a short stretch of that street, reduced to a cul-de-sac where the wall angled off, became a dump and produced an important pottery group. Other streets in this sector saw a variety of vicissitudes: thus *cardo* V did not exist north of *decumanus* VI in the latest periods, while *cardo* IV did not exist south of *decumanus* VI. Although *decumanus* VI at this point was only about 2.5 meters wide in the fifth or sixth century (at an earlier date it may not have existed here at all), a subsequent demolition of buildings on either side of it made it considerably wider. Both *decumanus* VI and *cardo* IV showed at least four further surfaces (sixth century or later).

Both of the houses immediately inside the wall between *cardines* II and III were abandoned at some date, probably in the late fifth or early sixth century, but by the seventh century intensive occupation had resumed. The house near the angle of *decumanus* VI and *cardo* II (house 2) was abandoned by the late fifth to early sixth century. Then in the seventh century the site was deliberately leveled by a thick layer of fill (compare the D phase at the British wall site) immediately inside the city wall, suggesting that access to the back of the wall was no longer required. Subsequently two plaster surfaces (*intervallum* road?) were put down on top of the leveling; although it is unclear whether they extended up against the rear of the city wall, they may well have done, like building 2 on the British wall site (E phase). Both surfaces evidently belonged to the seventh century, although a problematic Islamic sherd came from the bedding of one. Farther east two more similar surfaces were found behind the wall, again suggesting an *intervallum* road. There the lower one may have been sixth century, the resurfacing seventh century. In the gap between the city wall and a new north wall of a second house (house 1) located at the corner of *decumanus* VI and *cardo* III, another thick destruction level, with pottery dating up to the late sixth to early seventh century was found (compare British wall site, D phase). The reoccupation of the site (again probably seventh century) reused old wall foundations in places, but elsewhere placed walls directly on top of the earlier fourth century mosaics. The superstructure of these walls will have been of mudbrick with timber framing. A new drain was built leading out of the house into the sewer of *cardo* III, evidently still in operation. Another break in the occupation seems to have fallen before the final (fourth) phase (compare British wall site G phase) when shallow walls were placed on a spread of earth which in turn sealed the earlier mosaics. Earth floors and a hearth characterized this phase, but another drain was built leading into a newly built sewer of *cardo* III. By the seventh century the east wall of this house had encroached onto *cardo* III by about 1.65

meters from the line of the street frontage of the fourth century, when the street had still been about 6 meters wide.

The history of these and other areas directly inside the line of the new city wall thus seems to have been influenced directly by factors relating to the city's defense. In particular, much seems to have depended upon whether the defenses were being maintained and on whether a need was felt for access by means of an open space immediately inside the wall, between the wall and the built-up area. When the wall was constructed on both the British and Canadian II sites, it was built hard up against standing walls with no attempt made to demolish structures for any distance inside the wall to facilitate access. If that had been intended in ca. 425, the wall would have been placed a short distance in front of the existing buildings rather than abutted against them. However, at a later date it appears that the need was felt for space inside the wall to facilitate access. The exact date should be determined by evidence from both sites. We know that the city defenses were left abandoned during much of the Vandal period, but were put back into operation during the Byzantine period by Belisarius (Procopius, *de aedificiis* 6. 5; *de bello Vandalico* 23. 19–20). Thus, one can hypothesize that the houses up against the wall went out of use naturally during the later Vandal period and that in the early Byzantine period access was felt to be needed around the inside of the wall (perhaps this was also responsible for the late widening of *decumanus* VI on the north side and for the extra space created for *cardo* III, which must then have served as a main approach to the northern defenses in this sector), and that the rebuilding and reoccupation of the structures directly inside the wall occurred during the more tranquil and prosperous years of the late sixth and first half of the seventh centuries when the defenses had again fallen into disrepair. In that case phase III for the house between *decumanus* VI and *cardo* III would fall in the late sixth or early seventh century, following some decades of abandonment of the site, and phase IV would be late seventh century or later. Certainly we can say that this sector of the city, no less than others, saw intensive occupation during the seventh century.

The picture emerges, hazily to be sure, of a number of radical transformations in this region adjacent to the city wall at several moments between 425 and the end of the seventh century. More precision in the dating will help elucidate the factors that brought about these changes. Clearly the area was directly affected on several occasions by considerations dictated not by the inhabitants of these particular buildings but by those who controlled the city. Thus, in these cases perhaps better than in many other buildings in the city, the changes in the history of structures may be more closely and more confidently explained in connection with wider historical questions rather than simply on an individual building-by-building basis. The history of the two wall sectors thus seems to have had many points of similarity; the only important difference is the evident absence of (and lack of need for) an exterior ditch or ditches below the bluff on the north side (as confirmed also by the Italian excavations a little to the west). Evidently the southern defenses were considered the most vulnerable and therefore received greater attention at the various phases of their reinstatement.

A more representative picture of the fortunes of domestic housing in the city through this period is provided by the wealthiest private house so far examined, the House of the Greek Charioteers, located in the *insula* bounded by *decumani* II and III south and *cardines* VIII and IX east (University of Michigan excavation).[19] Constructed in the first quarter of the fifth century as an elaborate late Roman peristyle house, it went through several phases each marked by new floors, usually mosaics. In the porticoes two repavings with mosaic are presumably to be placed in the Vandal period (one in the second half of the fifth century, the other in the early sixth century) since they fall between those associated with the original construction of the house and the sixth century reconstruction. It was evidently also during the second half of the fifth century that the house encroached by about 1.6 meters into the area of the former street, taking over what seems to have been a former plastered sidewalk. The only hint of a period of discontinuity in the occupation of the house comes at around the time of the Byzantine conquest. Pottery from a pit dug in front of the entrance to the *triclinium* dated to the early sixth century, and the ledge which marked the southern edge of the courtyard was also robbed at about the same time. Several walls (and thus presumably also roofs) had collapsed and had to be rebuilt, normally on the same footings. Whether the house was abandoned by its occupants in the early sixth century is difficult to say. Although we originally dated the new mosaics and the elaborate *opus sectile* floor which was put down in the *triclinium* to soon after the Byzantine reconquest, evidence from the room just south of the *triclinium*, excavated in 1977, suggests that some reconstruction might date instead to the late sixth or early seventh century, which might mean that some parts of the house at least were abandoned during much of the sixth century.

The mosaics which are attributed to the Vandal period were not put down in the most important rooms and the fact that they all seem to have been geometric should not be taken as suggesting that no figured work in mosaics was done at that period. The geometric fragments which survive show competent workmanship and in many respects are indistinguishable from earlier geometric mosaics at Carthage. The *opus sectile* floor was of a high standard of execution, using expensive materials (stones from Egypt, Greece, and the Aegean) although a fair number of them may have been reused. This floor, which had a dominating central panel, a circle-in-square motif surrounded by borders and then by a separate frame with its own borders, recalls the use of *opus sectile* for wall decoration in some of the fifth and sixth century churches of Italy. The frame with its disks alternating with rectangles framed by volutes is particularly unusual.[20] The floor saw two later sets of repair, one dated later than a coin of Heraclius, and the house was evidently occupied at least until about the middle of the seventh century, although in the final phase (dated roughly to the first half of the seventh century) mortar and earth floors replaced the earlier mosaics, and there is evidence that some of the colonnades were walled up. There is also evidence for both a sixth and a seventh century robbing of walls in the house. It will be of interest to see whether the Byzantine reconstruction of this house can be linked closely in time to the construction of the new basilica directly across the street *cardo* IX.

A lower class commercial and domestic quarter of this period is well represented by the British excavations on the north side of the circular harbor.[21] There the *insula* between *cardines* XV and XVI east contained several structures (termed "units") of which nine have been identified. Its frontage toward the water, originally colonnaded or arcaded, also faced an open paved area which extended up to the Roman quay. Unlike the more common large residential dwellings centered around a peristyle, the structures there consisted of small units (in some cases "striphouses") which probably served both the residential and the commercial needs of lower class families. Relatively dense occupation is indicated by the frequency of cisterns, added at various dates through the Roman and later periods. Whether ownership of the block remained in the hands of one landlord, or whether the residents owned their own "unit," is unclear. Although in its earlier Roman phase the structures had *opus Africanum* walls, for most of its life relatively cheap building materials were used with mudbrick superstructures on stone sills and with floors that saw frequent patching (mosaics were rare). There is also evidence for ovens or hearths and for other temporary fittings in some rooms.

The *insula* saw a striking continuity of function and usage from

Roman to Byzantine times, despite the many internal modifications and additions that were made. It continued to function as small units with the same general boundary lines (except where encroachment on the streets occurred). There is general evidence for a comprehensive Byzantine re-building (presumably following a collapse or demolition), characterized according to the excavators by masonry using gray, charcoal-flecked mortar (a mortar-mixing area was also found); evidently at the same time the street and quayside frontages were altered, encroaching into the former public areas by about 2 meters and encasing what had been the colonnade facing the harbor. At the same period a paved alleyway was built leading halfway into the *insula* from *cardo* XVI (which was also re-made at this time); the alleyway is dated later than the early sixth century by coins and pottery in its makeup. It seems to have been designed to provide access directly to a row of five rooms presumably of a commercial nature which could all open directly on to it. The alleyway may have been entered through a gate off the street. The cisterns remained in use, with new inflow and outflow channels constructed in some cases. Earth floors with occupation layers above them characterize these late phases, and there is also evidence for stakeholes. At a later date one of the earlier cisterns was converted into a room with an earth floor entered by a door in the south side. The pottery from the site ran into the seventh century but the latest levels rarely survived. Earth surfaces found running over the Roman quay wall suggested that a new Byzantine quay wall may have been built farther out into the former harbor, paralleling what happened on the island. An infant burial in a stone cist was also cut into the earlier Roman quay wall.

The precise chronology of the phases that preceded the Byzantine rebuilding remains to be worked out, but at least some of the units seem to have been demolished and covered with thin earth spreads prior to the rebuilding. In view, however, of the general continuity of function, any interruption or break in occupation may have been relatively short-lived.

On the German site, which lies close to the modern shoreline just north of the *decumanus maximus*, an artisan and commercial quarter has been excavated. Like the British site on the north side of the circular harbor, this area also saw continuity from Roman to later periods, and no real changes occurred in the Vandal period. However, at this period, the upkeep of buildings began to be neglected and the robbing of walls made its first appearance, paralleling the situation on several other sites. In the sixth century a new phase of construction became necessary. The western edge of *cardo* XVII was abandoned and the sidewalks were encroached upon, although streets remained open. In the *insulae* there is important evidence for the reorganization of the water supply, which Rakob has suggested may have been the result of the interruption of the Zaghouan aqueduct. Some new large vaulted cisterns were installed. New walls were built following the partial robbing of Roman walls, but were sometimes built adjacent to rather than directly on top of the earlier lines. The latest walls on the site, of the seventh century, lack mortar or foundations, employ reused demolition material, and are often founded on earlier robber trenches (paralleling what happens in the Michigan ecclesiastical complex). A Byzantine workshop engaged in the production of bronze medallions and appliques has been found, and the commercial character of the area remained the same to the late seventh century.

One of the best sealed (and most intriguing) deposits from the Vandal period may prove to come from the Danish excavations (under S. Dietz) located on the coast north of the city wall at what seems to have been an elaborate Roman villa facing the sea.[22] There seem to have been two buildings there, set on slightly different alignments: one, which stepped back up the hillside, was supported partly on a line of vaulted substructures or chambers that were used initially for various domestic purposes. The other, at the foot of the slope, included at least two large rooms paved with elaborate mosaics, including the mosaic with a sea god (Oceanus and Nereids) found by Falbe and now in the British and Copenhagen museums. According to the excavators, this building was later than the set of vaulted chambers to the north, although not much later than the second half of the second century.

Of greatest interest is the publication of the material found in two rooms of the range of four in the upper western range. Both rooms were reused when tombs or mass graves were cut through the earlier floors during the last period of their history. The remains of thirty individuals were found in the southern room (called AO) and five in the north (AG), with one additional infant in front of the entrance (the skeletons are analyzed by B. Frohlich and D. Koplanski). In the south room the thirty individuals were placed in three layers; in the upper layer were six adults lying on their backs with their heads to the south; 10 cm below were seven adults again on their backs but with their heads to the west; third, confined to the southwest corner of the room, there were seven very young infants. The remains of ten other individuals (seven infants and three adults) could not be clearly linked with particular layers. In the northern room four skeletons lay on their backs facing east, one on its right side facing west. Overall the adults were placed on their backs, their feet close together, the left hand and left forearm placed on the left part of the body, the right hand and forearm placed beside the right side of the body. Generally infants were placed at random. An analysis of the skeletons by age showed that ten were about one year old, four were between one and five years, seven were between twenty and thirty years, four were between thirty and forty years, and six were over forty years old. Four more adults could not be closely aged. Of those identifiable by sex, eleven were males, and four were females; however, since six adults were unidentifiable by sex and two of those assigned to males were not secure, there remains the theoretical possibility that there was in this mass grave a relatively normal distribution between males and females. On average the men were about 5 feet 4 inches in height, the women 5 feet. The deliberate and consistent positioning of the adults points to a ritual or symbolic significance. It would be of interest to collect parallels from Vandal and Byzantine North Africa for burial practices of this kind. Orientation is here of less significance in a confined setting where substructures are being employed in lieu of digging a mass grave. A parallel for this practice comes from a cistern at Benghazi that contained forty-four skeletons and is dated to the early third century (J. A. Lloyd, ed., *Excavations at Sidi Khrebish Benghazi [Berenice]*, 1: 99).

Of particular interest are the causes of death and the date of this mass burial. Few traces of illness or disease could be detected on the skeletons and none likely to have been fatal. Most of the adults showed signs of rheumatism, particularly in the cervical and lumbar areas. The teeth in general were in good condition. Neither was there any trace of violence on the skeletons that might have pointed to death in warfare. Thus the likeliest interpretation seems to be that they died as the result of an epidemic or famine. In this connection the authors point out that no skeletons are present that belong to the age range five to twenty: thus the age group best able to resist plague or famine is absent. A radioisotope examination will be conducted to see whether there are differences in the bone mineral content of the bones, and thus possible evidence for famine as a cause.

More problematic is the date of the mass burial. In the smaller room AG (which is described and published in more detail), there were several layers over the skeletons. Almost all the skeletons were found in the lowest level excavated to date (AG 2,3), a sandy lighter layer with some largish fragments of plaster, some charcoal, iron rivets, and complete pottery vessels clearly serving as grave goods with the burials. These complete vessels were almost exclusively late Roman buff ware jugs.

Under the skull of one was a fourth to fifth century Roman coin, while a Vandal coin was found between the ribs of another skeleton. A lead plaque was found on the left shoulder of one. The large number of iron rivets suggested that there may have been wood coffins, although it seems unlikely that all the skeletons were originally coffined. Above the layer with the skeletons were two layers AG 2,2 and AG 2,1, which seem also to be contemporary with the burial and to have been placed on top of the burials by those responsible for the burial itself. Both contained a good deal of clay, presumably introduced here in order to seal the burials (a practice common to other cultures) as well as gray sand and ash, charcoal, stones, small fragments of plaster and a good number of animal bones (which one need not assume to have been connected with the burial but could have been redeposited from nearby on the site). The pottery from these layers that sealed the whole burial included the late Roman cookware type I of the Michigan classification, a late Roman amphora type 3, and African red slip ware Hayes's form 97 and a form close to 93A, as well as late Roman buff ware type 2. There is nothing in this pottery assemblage that needs to date later than the fifth century. (We might note, however, that if these levels contained primarily redeposited material, we might expect the pottery fragments from them to be slightly earlier rather than later than the grave goods proper.) At a higher level again within the same room were additional layers (AG 2, AG 3a, AG 2e2, and AG 2e1) that lacked the clay of the layers below and consisted mainly of stones and debris, mixed with charcoal, lime and mortar fragments, and animal bones. In these layers the range of pottery seemed to be greater: thus AG 2 contained African red slip form 104 (sixth century), flanged bowl type I (late fifth to mid-sixth century), late painted wares, a possible fragment of late Roman cookware type IV (perhaps seventh century), and another piece that may well be sixth century. The uppermost layer contained two examples of a flanged bowl type II (second half of sixth century). It was following the deposit of the last of these layers that the vault over the room caved in.

In their study of the finds, the Danish team grouped together the finds from all these layers, from the layer in which the skeletons rested to the topmost layer before the roof collapse, without differentiating the finds according to layer, and proceeded to argue, from the assumption that all this material should be contemporary and should date to the time of the burials, that the dates assigned to various types by J. W. Hayes need to be reconsidered (particularly the types listed above) since they are too late. Given the difference in the composition of these layers (particularly the clay division mentioned above), the burden of proof surely lies with the Danish excavators to show that all these layers were indeed deposited at the same moment. There can be no assumption that material was never subsequently dumped into these rooms between the moment of the burials and the time of the roof collapse (the rooms were never again covered with a solid floor). Indeed, the evidence indicates that a collapse in an adjacent room occurred later than a coin of A.D. 591–92, while Byzantine coins are relatively common from the site as a whole. Thus, it is clear that the site was not completely abandoned from the time when the burials were made, although later occupation may have been restricted to small sectors of the complex. We may however note that the latest forms of ARS (107 and 109) and other definitely seventh century sherds are absent from the levels in the room AG, suggesting that the vault collapse occurred prior to the late seventh century.

In short, the evidence of the pottery (viz. the grave goods themselves and the pottery finds in the layers immediately sealing the burials) seems to be consistent with a date in the late fifth century or soon after for the mass burial. The Vandalic coin found with one skeleton, if correctly attributed, and if a *nummus* as one assumes, would point to a date in the very last part of the fifth century, since the Vandals are not known to have struck bronze earlier than ca. 484, although it might have been struck at any time up to 533, which suggests that we cannot rule out the possibility that the burial dates to the very end of the Vandal period or even slightly later. One would have more confidence in saying that the burial is Vandal rather than early Byzantine if the coins had been studied in a more satisfactory manner. The breakdown of the coins from the site employs divisions that are incomprehensible, namely categories of "Roman coins of the 4th and 5th centuries," "Roman or Vandal coins of the 5th-6th c.," or "Vandal coins of the 5th c.," etc. What we need to know—since most of these coins are presumably illegible and only attributable by size—is which coins are *aes* 4 and which are *nummi*. One has the impression that all *nummi* are blanketed together as "Vandal coins of the 5th c.," despite the fact that *nummi* continued to be minted at Carthage until the end of the *sixth century*. Unattributable Vandal *nummi* are impossible to distinguish from unattributable Byzantine *nummi*. One also has the impression that the only coins termed "Byzantine" are coins larger in denomination than one *nummus*, in which case the overall picture of Byzantine coins from the site is being seriously underestimated, since in all levels of the sixth and seventh centuries at Carthage it is precisely the *nummi* that are present to be recovered by excavators

in the largest numbers. Thus the evidence of the coins, as published
so far, does not warrant the statement that "si nous en tenons aux
trouvailles de monnaies, le creusement du tombeau ne peut, d'au-
cune manière, être postérieur à env. 500 ap. J.-C." (Dietz and Trolle, p.
101). The evidence of the pottery directly associated with the burials and
in the layers which immediately seal the burials, however, does support
a date in the late fifth century or shortly after, since the later sherds only
occur in higher levels.

The upper layers in the other room (AO) were recognized as being
different from that of the burial proper. They were described as erosion
layers and contained much less carbon, debris, and bones than did the
upper layers in AG. Many coins (84) were found as well as a group of
pottery (including seven more complete jugs and an example of ARS
91A) in the northwest corner of the room opposite the entrance. Fourteen
pieces of pottery are published but there is no chronological discussion.
The coins are classed as Roman (A.D. 337–450) 19, 4th c. Roman 27, 5th c.
Roman-Vandal 14, 5th c. Vandal 20. Again, the category of "Vandal 5th
c." seems misleading, since it presumably includes *nummi* that could be
later than fifth century. However, a coin of Theodosius (402–50) was
found in the right hand of one skeleton, giving a firm *terminus post quem*,
and in general the high percentage of fourth century and other Roman
coins present may again suggest that the mass burials should not date
much later than the late fifth century or thereabouts. Thus, it becomes
even more likely that this is a mass burial from the Vandal period.

Finally, two general topics that pertain to many of the sites deserve
brief discussion. Encroachment of buildings onto streets has been detected by many of the teams. On the Michigan site *cardo* IX east was
evidently encroached upon during roughly the second half of the fifth
century, the area of the former plastered sidewalk being covered. The
Italian team has reported encroachment of *decumanus* V north and *cardo* II
west at the end of the fifth century. On the Byrsa the *cardo maximus*,
originally over 11 meters wide with a portico added in the second century
A.D., saw its portico walled up in the fourth or fifth century followed by
walls encroaching onto the street perhaps in the sixth century according
to the excavators, and occupation over much of the *cardo* in the sixth and
seventh centuries. On the British site on the north side of the circular
harbor, encroachment on *cardines* XV and XVI has been dated to the Byzantine period, while the Germans also claim that encroachment on their site
should be placed in the sixth century. *Cardo* III east on the second Canadian site was encroached upon by 1.65 meters by the seventh century. In

rare instances some streets may have been widened, as may have occurred with *decumanus* VI north just inside the Theodosian Wall on the
same Canadian site. The earlier Polish report that the *cardo maximus* was
widened in late antiquity, however, should be regarded as a misinterpretation of the evidence of their resistivity readings and small probe. A
reexamination of the evidence for encroachments on *decumanus* V north
on the first Canadian site[23] suggests that there was more than one such
encroachment: it appears that there was a series of encroachments from
the *insula* north of the Circular Monument. In the latest phase, probably
Byzantine, the width was reduced to only a little more than 3 meters.
It is also particularly interesting to observe the rise in the elevation
of the street surfaces: about 1.9 meters from the earliest to the latest.
There was a corresponding rise in the surfaces within the adjacent building to the north. The elevations of the latest street surfaces, dated later
than coins of Justinian, are also important for an interpretation of the
Circular Monument itself which stood on the south side of this *decumanus* at the north end of its *insula*. The evidence from the west end of
the ecclesiastical complex on the Michigan site also suggested that there
was a succession of three walls fronting the street, of which the first and
innermost was the earliest and the second perhaps was associated with
the ecclesiastical complex in one of its early phases. The basilica in this
insula also encroached slightly upon *cardo* X east as its apse projected
into the west half of that street.

The picture regarding encroachment is thus more complicated than
one might have suspected: it appears that encroachment did not occur at
all sites at precisely the same time. It looks as if the process was begun in
about the late fourth or early fifth centuries, perhaps resulting directly
from the many new churches which, because of their required east-west
axis, normally needed more than the 35 meter east-west length available
within the *insulae* of the city. Thus a precedent may have been set
whereby the church was permitted to encroach onto streets, perhaps
even blocking them completely in some instances (*cardo* II east by the
Circular Monument and its associated structures?). At an earlier date
only major public buildings had been permitted to embrace more than a
single *insula*—one thinks of the massive terrace incorporating the best
part of eight *insulae* on the Byrsa, or the theater and odeon which also
interrupted *cardines*. Once encroachment was allowed to begin, it seems
quickly to have become widespread from the fifth century onward. What
are the implications of such an event? Does it point to lax law enforcement

and a breakdown in the city's administration of public works thus suggesting ineffective municipal control in the later Vandal period? Or was a municipal decision made to permit this action, at least to the extent of permitting sidewalks to be incorporated into properties on those streets that were no longer required as major thoroughfares? (One assumes that some streets were maintained at close to their full width for ease of circulation.) Whether the land was sold or leased, or whether the city simply turned a blind eye, it appears that encroachment was regularized in the Byzantine period as part of the general and far-reaching program of municipal public works that also involved heavy expenditures in repaving streets and rebuilding the sewers of the city: most sites have produced evidence for major sixth century repaving of streets and rebuilding of sewers, both during the reign of Justinian and later; in many instances repairs continued to be made well into the seventh century. The last stage in the story evidently arrived only at the end of the seventh century, when rough structures were permitted to spread even farther over streets, in some cases blocking them completely, as may be true for *cardo* X east on the Michigan site and perhaps also for the *cardo maximus* on the Byrsa.

The second general topic is that of late burials within the city. Most of the teams now working at Carthage have evidence of this phenomenon. In this instance the intramural burials should always be distinguished from extramural burials such as those found by the Danish team or those outside the city wall found by the British and Italian teams. Intramural burials have been found on the two harbor sites, the north side of the circular harbor, the Michigan site (both in the ecclesiastical complex and on the south side of the House of the Greek Charioteers), on the British site immediately inside the city wall, and on both the Canadian sites. While in the case of the Circular Monument the possibility is not to be ruled out that burials were connected with the adjacent basilica, on most of the other sites there is no necessary connection with any Christian building. Most of the burials fall late in the stratigraphic sequence, although one baby burial from the Michigan ecclesiastical complex is no later than sixth century and possibly fifth century, and some on the island may be fifth century. Once again one is left with the impression of the breakdown of the old Roman laws about burial customs, which was probably due at least in part to the influence of the church at Carthage. Nevertheless, it seems that it was only in the seventh century that burials began to proliferate in odd places wherever there might be room. Most of the burials are cist graves, although amphora burials are also quite common. The burials are rarely accompanied by any significant grave goods, which may support the notion of a late date. The discovery of intramural burials on a site during the seventh century (probably second half in most cases) should not, however, be interpreted as evidence for a break in the domestic habitation of a site, or that large areas of the city had become depopulated and abandoned. In fact, the evidence from sites like the Michigan ecclesiastical complex tends to suggest that the city was densely inhabited during the second half of the seventh century.

Tentatively, a general outline based upon the current archaeological work can now be formulated. The late fourth and early fifth centuries was a time of great prosperity; an enormous amount of new building construction (including churches, public buildings, and private houses) was in progress, the spectacles in the entertainment buildings were as popular as ever, the old pagan religion continued to flourish, local industries like the mosaic and pottery workshops operated at a high level, and contacts with the east were strong. The city wall was then built in about 425, perhaps by Boniface during his period of military command in Africa.

The period of Vandal rule at Carthage seems to have been one of contrasts between public and private areas. Public areas like the twin harbors or the city wall seem to have become neglected and allowed to decay, finally falling prey to stone robbers in the later Vandal period. Churches and other ecclesiastical buildings also had a checkered history during this period and several may have passed completely out of use, again becoming targets for robbing. The beginnings of encroachment by buildings onto the public areas of streets also seems to become frequent in the Vandal period—often by almost 2 meters (sometimes by incorporating former sidewalks). The massive program of street and sewer repairs in the Byzantine period also implied some neglect in the later Vandal period. Private houses or commercial structures, on the other hand, may have suffered less during the Vandal rule: their owners or occupants seem to have made more of an effort to maintain them, even replacing worn out mosaic floors with new ones, and there is less sign of them falling into disrepair except in special circumstances as up against the city wall. Imports to the city from the eastern Mediterranean (especially of wines) continued to be strong and there are other indications of relative prosperity and continuity of civilized life, with the survival of many aspects of the late Roman world. In the later Vandal period shortly before or at the time of the reconquest, some houses may have been abandoned and allowed to decay or collapse and may not always have been put back into working operation immediately.

The Byzantine reconquest also produced a complicated chain of events. While there is evidence for attention to churches, by way of renovation, reconstruction, and completely new foundations, relatively early in the Byzantine period, all ecclesiastical buildings were not brought back into operation simultaneously. The revitalization of the churches marched hand in hand with the greatly increased powers of the bishops in civil affairs. There is also strong evidence for Byzantine attention to the city defenses and other public areas such as streets (new street sewers were normally built and streets repaired) and the twin harbors, which included the reconstruction of the quay walls and the re-monumentalization of these areas as impressive focal points of the waterfront. Whether the Byzantine plans for the harbors were ever completed remains open to question. The early Byzantine period also saw the reconstruction of some private houses and other commercial structures, and some systematization and rationalization of the problem of encroachment onto streets, which now seems to have become uniformly accepted and practiced throughout most of the city. We should, however, resist the temptation of supposing that most of the reconstruction occurred immediately after the conquest. Africa remained unsettled for much of Justinian's reign, and reconstruction proceeded at an uneven pace.

The first half of the seventh century stands out as one of intensive occupation in the ecclesiastical complex of the Michigan site, although it is too early to say whether the city as a whole experienced considerable economic prosperity at this time. Several sites, however, have produced evidence for reconstruction and a moderately high standard of living. Byzantine links with Carthage in the seventh century are well attested through imported pottery from Constantinople and Cyprus (late seventh century glazed ware I at Carthage perhaps copied the contemporary glazed ware of Constantinople) and from the evidence of the coinage. African red slip pottery continued to be produced perhaps right up to the end of the seventh century, although imported finewares had become very rare. At some time after the middle of the seventh century, there seems to have been a marked downturn in the fortunes of the city, perhaps to be associated with an exodus of some of the wealthier members of the community. Disturbance and robbing on many sites—frequently pointing to a break in the sequence of occupation—is attested, and the twin harbors were evidently abandoned and given over to private individuals who put up rough structures, buried their dead nearby, and operated pottery kilns. Intramural burials became much more common in the second half of the seventh century, normally cist graves oriented east-west with few if any grave goods. The final years of the city during the last quarter of the seventh century were marked on at least some sites by extraordinarily intense occupation within the shell of older buildings wherever possible, and where not, by falling back on their own resources, the occupants constructing flimsy structures with earth floors, wattle partitions, and mudbrick walls.

More detail about the economy of the city comes from faunal and environmental studies: throughout the Vandal and Byzantine periods sheep or goat seems to have been the most important food animal, with pig a very close and important second. Chicken and fish remained common food sources. In the latest part of the seventh century or later it appears that a larger number of young individuals were being killed, perhaps indicative of a period of stress where there were too many mouths to feed and not enough food. More information will come from the large sealed deposits from cisterns on the Michigan site and from dumps in the circular harbor, which range widely through the Vandal and Byzantine periods and are now being studied. Preliminary work by the Dutch team from the University of Groningen (under W. van Zeist) has established that by the Byzantine period deforestation had been pushed much further from the city than in earlier periods, and that pine was no longer present in the Carthage region. The area planted with wheat was much greater than in the Punic period.

The general outline, although still tentative and in many cases lacking firm, published dating evidence, is becoming clear despite the many variations and idiosyncrasies that each site exhibits. What is needed now is precision in dating the changes on each site, so that attempts to integrate the archaeological and historical record can be made more plausibly and with more confidence. Precision in dating will also be aided by the creation of a good corpus of dated walls, building materials, and mortars. (Does charcoal-flecked mortar, for example, really bear any precise chronological indications?) We need too to continue to reassess some of our old assumptions: there is now evidence for the continuity of mosaic production through the Vandal period into the Byzantine, for intensive activity throughout the first half of the seventh century (if not longer), and for the survival of many of the public buildings to a later date than was previously supposed, not to mention the fervent activity, coupled with a marked decline in building standards and perhaps also in economic conditions, in the last decade or two before the Arab conquest.

NOTES

The information presented in this chapter depends heavily upon the work of many colleagues, both members of the University of Michigan team at Carthage and those of the other teams working in the city. I have drawn extensively upon the published reports, both in the Michigan volumes (four published, two forthcoming) and elsewhere, as cited in the bibliography. I wish particularly to express my gratitude to those who have funded our work, the Foreign Currency Program of the Smithsonian Institution and the Kelsey Museum of the University of Michigan, our sponsoring institution the American Schools of Oriental Research, the fine array of specialists who have been members of the Michigan team during the last five years, and the supervisors who have toiled week after week on mudbrick tips and beaten earth compactions with cheerful resolve. It is the work of these supervisors and other excavators that has formed the backbone of our results. For particular help with the preparation of this paper and for providing many of the ideas which are included, I am most indebted to S. P. Ellis, assistant field director of the Michigan team, and R. B. Hitchner, numismatist.

1. This idea owes much to R. B. Hitchner and S. P. Ellis.

2. Once again my main debt is to S. P. Ellis in the section which follows.

3. H. Hurst, "Excavations at Carthage 1976: Third Interim Report," *AntJ* 56 (1976): 259.

4. S. Roskams and H. Hurst in H. Hurst, "Excavations at Carthage 1975: Second Interim Report," *AntJ* 55 (1975): 194.

5. S. P. Ellis, "Notes on Field Techniques and the Excavation of Robber Trenches at Carthage," in *Excavations at Carthage Conducted by the University of Michigan, 1976*, vol. 4, ed. J. H. Humphrey (Ann Arbor, 1978), pp. 17–18.

6. Roskams and Hurst in Hurst, "Excavations at Carthage 1975," p. 194, and S. P. Ellis, "The Ecclesiastical Complex: Stratigraphic Report 1976," in *Excavations at Carthage Conducted by the University of Michigan, 1976*, vol. 3, ed. J. H. Humphrey (Ann Arbor, 1976), p. 67.

7. J. H. Humphrey, "A Discussion of the Interpretation of the Numismatic Evidence in the Context of the History of the Site," in *Michigan*, vol. 4, pp. 164–68.

8. R. B. Hitchner in *Excavations at Carthage Conducted by the University of Michigan, 1977*, vol. 5, ed. J. H. Humphrey, (Ann Arbor, 1980), pp. 261–69.

9. T. V. Buttrey and R. B. Hitchner, "The Coins—1976," in *Michigan, 1976*, vol. 4, p. 101.

10. This discussion of Vandal coinage owes much to R. B. Hitchner.

11. S. P. Ellis in *Michigan, 1977*, vol. 5, chap. 2.

12. The cisterns on the Michigan site and their contents are discussed fully in *Excavations at Carthage Conducted by the University of Michigan, 1977*, vol. 6 (forthcoming).

13. The phasing of the ecclesiastical complex has been worked out by S. P. Ellis in *Michigan, 1976*, vol. 3, pp. 41–67, and *Michigan, 1977*, vol. 5, pp. 7–123. This summary is drawn from those chapters.

14. For preliminary reports on the Circular Monument, see P. Senay, F. Beaulieu, M. Beauregard, M. Gazaille, and L. Guimond, *Carthage I: rapport préliminaire Carthage 1976*, Cahiers des études anciennes no. 6 (Montreal, 1976); P. Senay and M. Beauregard, *Carthage II: rapport préliminaire Carthage 1978*, Cahiers des études anciennes no. 9 (Montreal, 1978); and P. Senay, "Carthage 1978: fouilles du monument circulaire," *EMC/CNV* 23, no. 1 (January 1979): 9–14.

15. This summary is based upon the three interim reports by H. Hurst: Hurst, "Excavations at Carthage: First Interim Report," *AntJ* 55 (1975): 11–40; Hurst, "Excavations at Carthage 1975"; Hurst, "Excavations at Carthage 1976."

16. This summary is based upon the preliminary reports of L. E. Stager: L. E. Stager, "Excavations at Carthage 1975, the Punic Project: First Interim Report," *American Schools of Oriental Research Annual* 43 (1978):151–90; L. E. Stager, "Carthage 1977: The Punic and Roman Harbors," *Archaeology* 30, no. 3 (1977):198–200; L. E. Stager, "The Punic Project," *The Oriental Institute Annual Report* (1977–78): 27–36.

17. See H. Hurst, "Excavations at Carthage 1975," pp. 255–59; "Excavations at Carthage 1976," pp. 193–96.

18. See C. M. Wells and E. M. Wightman, "Carthage 1978: la muraille Theodosienne," *EMC/CNV* 23, no. 1 (1979): 15–18, and C. M. Wells and E. M. Wightman, "Canadian Excavations at Carthage, 1976 and 1978: The Theodosian Wall, Northern Sector," *JFA* 7 (1980): 43–63.

19. The house is discussed in *Excavations at Carthage Conducted by the University of Michigan, 1975*, vol. 1, ed. J. H. Humphrey (Tunis, 1976), chap. 1; *Excavations at Carthage Conducted by the University of Michigan, 1975*, vol. 2, ed. J. H. Humphrey (Ann Arbor, 1978), chap. 2; *Michigan, 1976*, vol. 3, chap. 5; and in forthcoming vols. 6 and 7.

20. The mosaics are discussed by K. M. D. Dunbabin in *Michigan, 1975*, vol. 1, chap. 2. The marbles used in the *opus sectile* floor are analyzed by R. G. Bullard in *Michigan, 1975*, vol. 2, chap. 3.

21. See interim reports by H. Hurst and, particularly, Hurst, "Excavations at Carthage 1976."

22. See E. Anderson et al., "Nye danske volgravninger : Oldtidens Karthago," *Nationalmuseets Arbejdsmark* (1978), pp. 50–64; and S. Dietz and S. Trolle, *Premier rapport préliminaire sur les fouilles danoises à Carthage*, National Museum of Denmark Working Papers, no. 10 (1979).

23. See P. Senay, *Carthage II*, especially plan II.

APPENDIX
Carthage in the Age of Augustine: The Pottery Evidence

John W. Hayes

A reassessment of the dating of the pottery of the period about A.D. 380–450 is made necessary by finds from the recent American, Canadian, and British excavations at Carthage. Dates approximately twenty to twenty-five years earlier than those published in *Late Roman Pottery* (London, 1972) are now preferable for the Carthage series of African red slip ware of this period; later fifth century datings also require some adjustment. To an earlier revision proposed in *Roman Pottery Studies in Britain and Beyond (British Archaeological Reports*, Supp., 30 (1977): 269–77) is added material from a recently found deposit from the Canadian excavations (about to appear in *Antiquités Africaines*) and from Fulford's type-series from the British excavations (report in press). Certain types of imported amphorae, mainly of Eastern origin, are also examined. The characteristic Byzantine amphora types of the fifth and sixth centuries are shown to have first appeared in Carthage between about 390 and 430 (however, see M. Egloff in *Kellia*, vol. 3, for slightly earlier occurrences in Egypt). Further refinements in the dating of these types of pottery are to be expected shortly.

In deference to the authors of reports now in press, this paper is not published in full.

Bibliography of the
International Campaign to Save Carthage

John H. Humphrey

For up-to-date summaries of the ongoing work, readers should consult the *CEDAC Bulletin* (Institut National d'Archéologie et d'Art de Tunisie), no. 1 (September 1978) and subsequent issues.

Andersen, E.; Dietz, S.; Kromann, A.; Lund, J.; and Trolle, S. "Nye danske udgravninger i Oldtidens Karthago." *Nationalmuseets Arbejdsmark* (1978): 50–64.

Boyadjiev, S. "La rotonde souterraine de Damous el Karita à Carthage à la lumière de nouvelles données." *Atti IX Cong. Int. di Archeologia Cristiana* 2 (1975): 117–30 (with discussion pp. 130–31).

Buhl, M.-L., and Dietz, S. "Karthago bør reddes." *Nationalmuseets Arbejdsmark* (1975): 183–85.

Caputo, G. "Attività archeologica in Libia, Algeria, Tunisia 1966–75." *Quaderni de "La ricerca scientifica,"* no. 100 (1978): 210–17.

Cunliffe, B. W. "Carthage," *Antiquity* 50, no. 198 (1976): 138–39.

Dietz, S., and Trolle, S. *Premier rapport préliminaire sur les fouilles danoises à Carthage: Les campagnes de 1975 et 1977.* National Museum of Denmark Working Papers, no. 10 (1979), containing:

Dietz, S. "Description préliminaire des vestiges—Datation."

Lund, J.; Balling, A. K.; Bro, T.; and Trolle, S. "Decouvertes d'objets en céramique et de pièces de monnaies."

Frölich, B., and Kopjanski, D. "Rapport préliminaire sur les squelettes excavés dans les tombeaux AG et AO."

Malcus, B. "Determinations préliminaires des inscriptions."

Andersen, E., and Dietz, S. "Appendices 1–2."

Ennabli, A. "Metodologia di scavo a Cartagine." *Enciclopedia della scienza e della technica mondadori* (annuario), 75: 233–40.

Hamblin, D. J. "Carthage." *Smithsonian Magazine* 9, no. 11 (February 1979): 42–55.

Humphrey, J. H. "North African Newsletter 1." *AJA* 82 (1978): 511–20.

Humphrey, J. H., ed. *Excavations at Carthage Conducted by the University of Michigan, 1975*. Vol. 1 (Tunis, 1976), containing:

Brown, R.; Humphrey, J. H.; and MacLennan, J. "Preliminary Field Report." Pp. 1–19.

Dunbabin, K. M. D. "The Mosaics and Pavements." Pp. 21–46.

Hayes, J. W. "Pottery: Stratified Groups and Typology." Pp. 47–123.

Riley, J. A. "The Carthage System for the Quantification of Pottery." Pp. 125–56.

Buttrey, T. V. "The Coins." Pp. 157–97.

Henig, M. "The Gemstones." Pp. 199–200.

Rosenberg, A. "The Conservation of Excavated Material from Carthage." Pp. 201–3.

————. *Excavations at Carthage Conducted by the University of Michigan, 1975*. Vol. 2 (Ann Arbor, 1978), containing:

Bullard, R. G. "The Environmental Geology of Roman Carthage." Pp. 3–25.

Brown, R., and Humphrey, J. H. "The Stratigraphy of the 1975 Season." Pp. 27–112.

Hayes, J. W. "Selected Pottery Deposits (continued)." Pp. 113–18.

Humphrey, J. H. "Locus List P_3." Pp. 119–65.

Bullard, R. G. "The Marbles of the *Opus Sectile* Floor." Pp. 167–86.

Hayes, J. W. "Glass Finds from the 1975 Season." Pp. 187–93.

Humphrey, J. H. "The Polish Archaeological and Geophysical Investigations at Carthage in 1972: A Review." Pp. 195–216.

Sidebotham, S. "Lamps from Carthage in the Kelsey Museum." Pp. 217–38.

Humphrey, J. H. "Carthage in 1925: The Photographs of George Swain." Pp. 239–40, 252–309.

————. *Excavations at Carthage Conducted by the University of Michigan, 1976*. Vol. 3 (Ann Arbor, 1977), containing:

Eadie, J. W., and Humphrey, J. H. "The Topography of the Southeast Quarter of Later Roman Carthage." Pp. 1–19.

Frend, W. H. C. "The Early Christian Church in Carthage." Pp. 21–40.

Ellis, S. P. "The Ecclesiastical Complex: Stratigraphic Report 1976." Pp. 41–67.

Humphrey, J. H., and Ellis, S. P. "Ecclesiastical Complex Locus Lists 1976." Pp. 69–94.

Humphrey, J. H. "Other Work in 1976." Pp. 95–115.

Vann, R. L. "A Discussion of the Cisterns." Pp. 116–29.

Reese, D. S. "Faunal Remains (Osteological and Marine Forms) 1975–76." Pp. 131–66.

Frend, W. H. C., and Humphrey, J. H. "Bronze Cross and Christian Inscriptions." Pp. 167–73.

———. *Excavations at Carthage Conducted by the University of Michigan, 1976.* Vol. 4 (Ann Arbor, 1978) containing:

Clover, F. M. "Carthage in the Age of Augustine." Pp. 1–14.

Ellis, S. P. "Notes on Field Techniques and the Excavation of Robber Trenches at Carthage." Pp. 15–22.

Hayes, J. W. (with tables by J. A. Riley). "Pottery report—1976." Pp. 23–98.

Buttrey, T. V., and Hitchner, R. B. "The Coins—1976." Pp. 99–163.

Humphrey, J. H. "A Discussion of the Interpretation of the Numismatic Evidence in the Context of the History of the Site." Pp. 164–68.

Dunbabin, K. M. D. (with sample descriptions by L. H. Davis). "The Pavement Fragments and their Typology." Pp. 169–80.

Ford, R. I., and Miller, N. "Paleoethnobotany I." Pp. 181–87. With an appendix by R. L. Vann, "The Contexts of the Building Mortar Samples." Pp. 188–89.

———. *Excavations at Carthage Conducted by the University of Michigan, 1977.* Vol. 5 (Ann Arbor, 1980), containing:

Duncan-Jones, R. P. "Age-Rounding in Roman Carthage." Pp. 1–6.

Ellis, S. P. "The Ecclesiastical Complex: Stratigraphic Report 1977." Pp. 7–124.

Vann, R. L. "Problems and Procedures in Architectural Recording at Carthage." Pp. 125–34.

Ellis, S. P., and Humphrey, J. H. "Ecclesiastical Complex Locus Lists 1977." Pp. 135–83.

Metcalf, W. E., and Hitchner, R. B. "The Coins—1977." Pp. 185–270.

Humphrey, J. H., and Pedley, J. G. "Roman Carthage." *Scientific American* 238 (January 1978): 111–20.

Hurst, H. "Excavations at Carthage 1974: First Interim Report." *AntJ* 55 (1975): 11–40.

———. "Excavations at Carthage 1975: Second Interim Report." *AntJ* 56 (1976): 177–97.

————. "Excavations at Carthage 1976: Third Interim Report." *AntJ* 57 (1977): 232–61.

Hurst, H., and Stager, L. E. "A Metropolitan Landscape: The Late Punic Port of Carthage." *World Archaeology* 9, no. 3 (1978): 334–46.

Iciek, A., et al. *Carthage: cirque—colline dite de Junon—Douar Chott, Recherches archéologiques et géophysiques polonaises effectuées en 1972.* Warsaw: Academie Polonaise des Sciences. 1974.

————. "Prospections géophysiques à Carthage." *Prospezioni Archeologiche* 9 (1974): 61–74.

Jentel, M.-O. "En marge des fouilles Canadiennes à Carthage: quelques scènes des légendes d'Achille et d'Héraclès." *Revue d'art Canadienne* 4, no. 1 (1977): 36–39.

Kolendo, J. "Quelques remarques sur le plan de Carthage à la lumière des recherches archéologiques et géophysiques polonaises." *Etudes et Travaux* 8 (1975).

Kuzmanov, G. "Etude du littoral de la Carthage romaine." *Archeologija* (Sofia) 18 (1976): 19–33.

Lancel, S. "Fouilles de Carthage 1976–1977: la colline de Byrsa et l'occupation punique." *CRAI,* 1978, pp. 300–331.

————. "Nouvelles fouilles de la mission archéologique française à Carthage sur la colline de Byrsa: Campagnes de 1974 et 1975." *CRAI,* 1976, pp. 60–78.

Lancel, S.; Deneauve, J.; and Carrié, J. M. "Fouillies françaises à Carthage (1974–1975)." *AntAfr* 11 (1977): 13–130.

Lancel, S., et al. *Byrsa 1: rapports préliminaires des fouilles (1974–1976).* Collection de l'école française de Rome, no. 41 (Rome, 1979), containing:

> Lancel, S., and Deneauve, J. "Un siècle de fouilles sur la colline de Byrsa: Historique des recherches."
>
> Lancel, S.; Carrié, J.-M.; Sanviti, N.; Deneauve, J.; and Villedieu, F. "Le Secteur A(1974–1975), le Secteur B(1974–1975), le *Cardo Maximus* et les édifices à l'est de la voie(1974–1976)."
>
> Lancel, S.; Thuillier, J.-P.; and Gros, P. "Les niveaux puniques et romains 1976."
>
> Saumagne, Ch. "Le Métroôn de Carthage et ses abords."
>
> Carrié, J.-M. "Un brule-parfums trouvé à Carthage."
>
> Thuillier, J.-P. "Un marque amphorique au nom de Magon, en grec."

Rakob, F., in *Archäologischer Anzeiger* 1975, p. 576; 1976, p. 524; 1977, p. 627. Short summaries of work.

Sarnowski, T. "En marge des résultats des recherches archéologiques et géophysiques poursuivies à Carthage par l'équipe polonaise." *Archeologia* (Warszawa) 26 (1975): 165–69.

Senay, P. "Carthage 1978: fouilles du monument circulaire." *EMC/CNV* 23 no. 1 (January 1979): 9–14.

Senay, P.; Beaulieu, F.; Beauregard, M.; Gazaille, M.; and Guimond, L. *Carthage I: rapport préliminaire Carthage 1976.* Cahier des études anciennes no. 6 (1976).

Senay, P., and Beauregard, M. *Carthage II: rapport préliminaire Carthage 1978.* Cahier des études anciennes no. 9 (1978).

Stager, L. E. "Carthage the Punic Project." *American Schools of Oriental Research Newsletter* 3-4 (October-November 1975): 10-11.

————. "Carthage 1977: The Punic and Roman Harbors." *Archaeology* 30, no. 3 (1977): 198-200.

————. "The Punic Project." *The Oriental Institute Annual Report* 1977-78. Pp. 27-36.

————. "Excavations at Carthage 1975, the Punic project: First Interim Report." *American Schools of Oriental Research Annual.* Vol. 43 (1978): 151-90.

UNESCO, *Projet Tunis-Carthage.* 1971.

The UNESCO Courier, "Carthage Must Not Be Destroyed," December 1970 (special issue).

Wells, C. M. "Carthage 1976: la muraille Théodosienne." *EMC/CNV* 21 (1977): 15-23.

Wells, C. M.; Neuru, L.; and Blockley, R. C. "Carthage, Site 2: The Theodosian Wall (with Appendices on the Pottery and Coins from the 1976 Excavations)." *EMC/CNV* 22 (1978): 9-12.

Wells, C. M., and Wightman, E. M. "Canadian Excavations at Carthage, 1976 and 1978: The Theodosian Wall, Northern Sector." *JFA* 7 (1980): 43-63.

————. "Carthage 1978: la muraille Théodosienne." *EMC/CNV* 23 (1979): 15-18.

Yorke, R. A. "Search for Submerged Carthage." *Geographical Magazine,* November 1976, pp. 24-28.

Yorke, R. A., and Little, J. H. "Offshore Survey at Carthage, Tunisia, 1973." *International Journal of Nautical Archaeology and Underwater Exploration* 4 (1975): 85-101.

Yorke, R. A.; Little, J. H.; and Davidson, D. P. "Offshore Survey of the Harbors of Carthage: Summary of 1975 Season's Work." *International Journal of Nautical Archaeology and Underwater Exploration* 5 (1976): 173-75.

Illustrations

Fig. 1–1. General view of the precinct looking east. The monuments, mostly cippi from late Tanit II, were exposed by the Kelsey excavations of 1925 and left standing in situ. The trench for areas 1–3 of the current ASOR excavations can be seen in the background to the left. In 1978–79 areas 5–6 continued the trench to the west where Kelsey had worked.

Fig. 1–2. Phase 1 urn with red-slipped and burnished bands on neck and waist of vessel, vertical line groups (black paint) between the bands.

Fig. 1–3.   Phase 4 (upper) urn in stone-lined pit cut into a phase 3 (lower) urn. Both urns are Tanit I types.

Fig. 1–4.   Phase 2 small sandstone cippus sits below later phase 7 cippi.

Fig. 1–5. Phase 8 micritic limestone stelae with gables. Typical wasp-waisted urn (Group B) lies to left and below center stela. Stela to right (partially in balk) has incised Punic inscription. Dedicant is Eshmun-hilles. Below the stela was a fourth century B.C. urn with a newborn baby in it.

Fig. 1–6. Various types of amulets that had once been strung on a necklace and placed in an urn along with the charred remains of a child. Note the seven circumcised phalli in lower row and three lead figurines in center row.

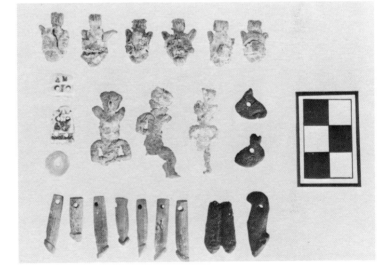

Fig. 1–7. Phase 4 sandstone cippus and urn below. This Tanit I-type urn contained *only* the charred bones of a lamb.

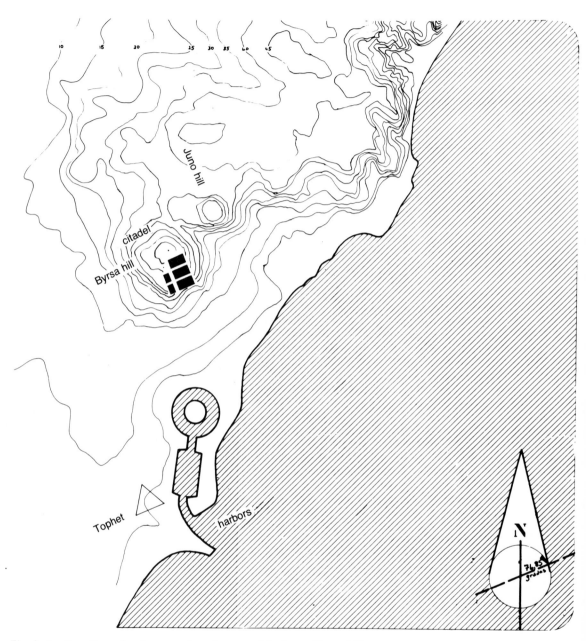

Fig. 2–1. Location of early second century B.C. blocks on Byrsa hill.
(*Original drawing by G. Robine.*)

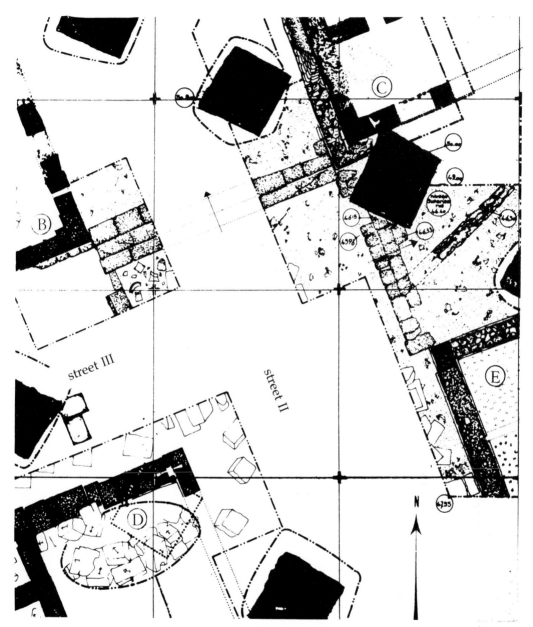

Fig. 2–2. Crossroad at the intersection of streets II and III. (*Original plan by G. Robine.*)

Fig. 2–3.   The steps on streets II and III. (*Photograph by S. Lancel.*)

Fig. 2–4.   The five blocks; schematic actual state plan and cross section northwest to southeast. (*Original plan by G. Robine.*)

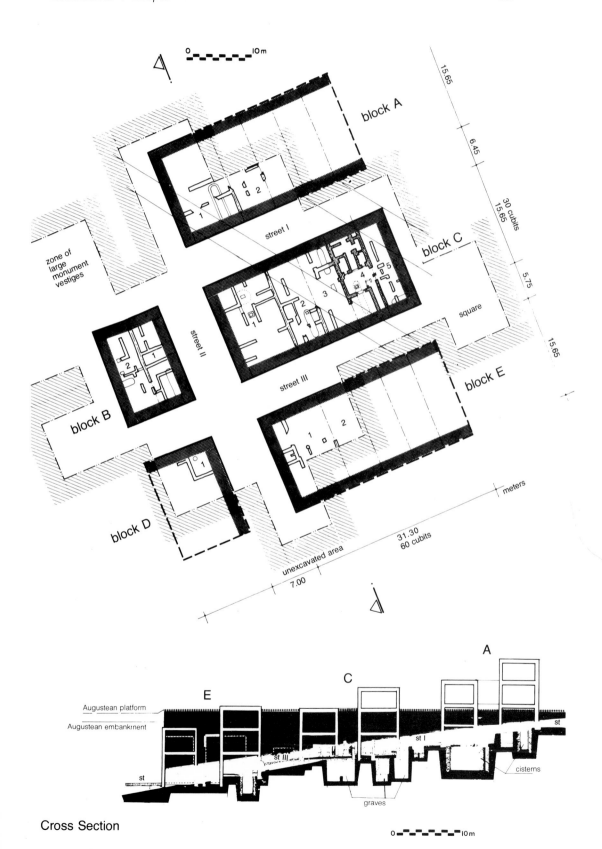

block A

street I

block C

15.65

6.45

30 cubits

15.65

5.75

15.65

square

zone of
large
monument
vestiges

street II

block B

street III

block E

block D

meters

unexcavated area

31.30
60 cubits

7.00

Cross Section

A

C

E

Augustean platform

Augustean embankment

st

st III

st I

st

cisterns

graves

0 10m

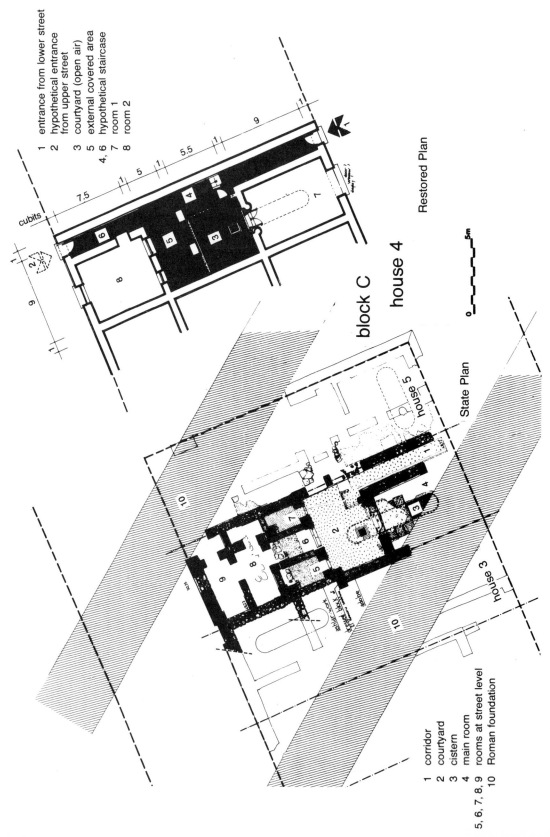

1 entrance from lower street
2 hypothetical entrance
   from upper street
3 courtyard (open air)
5 external covered area
4, 6 hypothetical staircase
7 room 1
8 room 2

cubits

Restored Plan

block C

house 4

State Plan

house 5

house 3

5m

1 corridor
2 courtyard
3 cistern
4 main room
5, 6, 7, 8, 9 rooms at street level
10 Roman foundation

Fig. 2–5. Block C: fourth house; state plan and restored plan. (*Original plan by G. Robine.*)

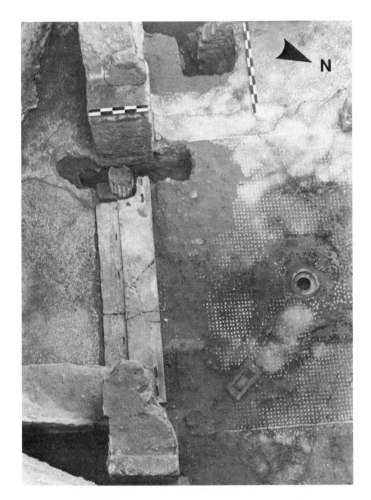

Fig. 2-6. Block E: courtyard with *impluvium* and outlet of the overflow pipe of the cistern; on the left side, threshold of the *oecus*. (*Photograph by S. Lancel.*)

Fig. 2-7. Northeast angle of block C., showing part of fifth house and the packing of rubble with waterproof coating on the outside face of the wall limiting the block. (*Photograph by S. Lancel.*)

Fig. 3-1. Topographic map 1976–78: excavations in relation to theoretical street grid.

Fig. 3–2. View from roof of apartment building astride *cardo* III, looking northwest: on the left, beyond trees, continuation of Teurf el-Sour west of *cardo maximus;* the field bank on the right between the trees and the road continues the line of *decumanus* IV. (*Photograph by E. Wightman.*)

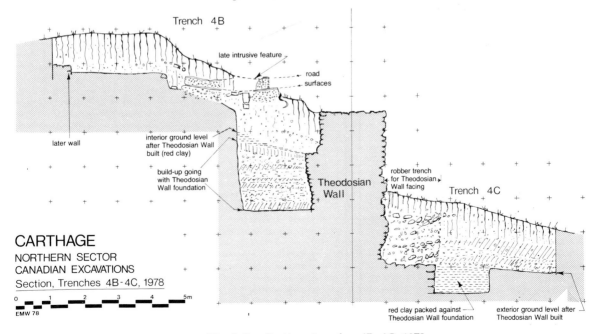

Trench 4B

late intrusive feature

road
surfaces

later wall

interior ground level
after Theodosian Wall
built (red clay)

build-up going
with Theodosian
Wall foundation

Theodosian
Wall

robber trench
for Theodosian
Wall facing

Trench 4C

CARTHAGE
NORTHERN SECTOR
CANADIAN EXCAVATIONS
Section, Trenches 4B-4C, 1978

0   1   2   3   4   5m

EMW 78

red clay packed against
Theodosian Wall foundation

exterior ground level after
Theodosian Wall built

Fig. 3–3. Section, trenches 4B–4C, 1978.

Fig. 3–4. View from roof of apartment building looking north toward
Damous el-Karita basilica, showing line of Teurf el-Sour between
cardo III (bottom left) and cardo IV. (*Photograph by C. Wells.*)

Fig. 3–5. View from roof of apartment building looking east,
showing Teurf el-Sour from *cardo* IV eastward, with trial excavations
2CC6 (bottom left) and 2CC5 (center). (*Photograph by E. Wightman.*)

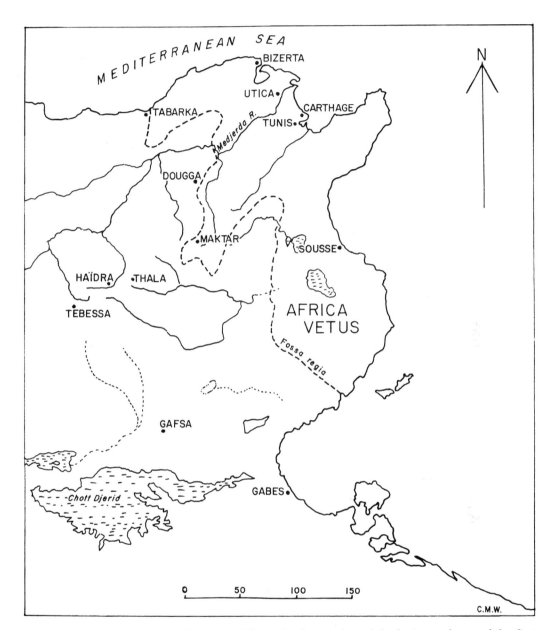

Fig. 4–1. Africa: the *fossa regia* and the legionary bases of the first century A.D.

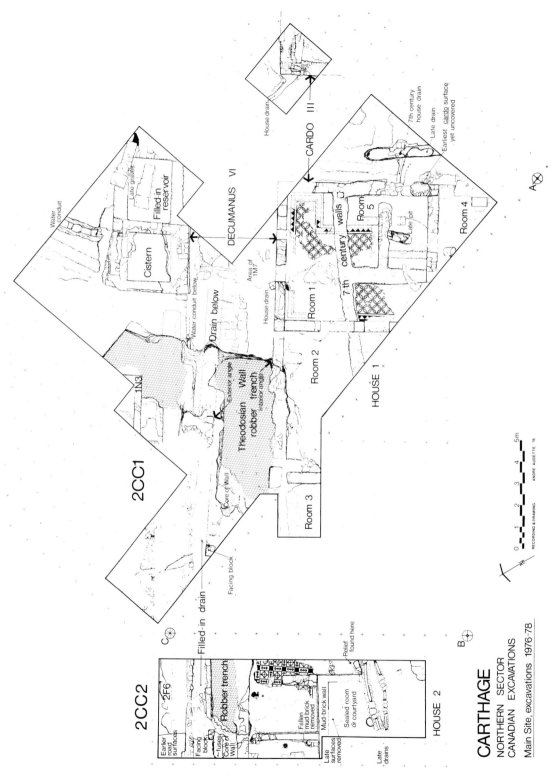

Fig. 4-2. Plan: main site (2CC1 and 2CC2), excavations 1976–78.

Fig. 4–3. 2CC1: Robber trench of Theodosian Wall, with remains of *decumanus* VI (right), showing arched drain beneath street. (*Photograph by C. Wells.*)

Fig. 4–4. 2CC1: View from *decumanus* VI looking west, showing remains of house 1 (left), robber trench (center), and filled-in drain with facing stone of Theodosian Wall in situ (right). (*Photograph by C. Wells.*)

Fig. 4-5. 2CC2: Overhead view of northern part of trench, showing (left to right) remains of house 2 (the outer wall of the house is directly above the photographer's foot), and narrower robber trench of Theodosian Wall, filled-in drain of *decumanus* VI, and remains of earlier levels. (*Photograph by William A. Graham.*)

Fig. 4-6. 2CC4: Outer face of core of Theodosian Wall, showing level of foundations and evidence for robbing of facing stones above foundation level. (*Photograph by E. Wightman.*)

Fig. 5–1. General view of the site from south. (*Photograph by William A. Graham.*)

Fig. 5–2. Plan IX from *Carthage II:* Elias Markou.

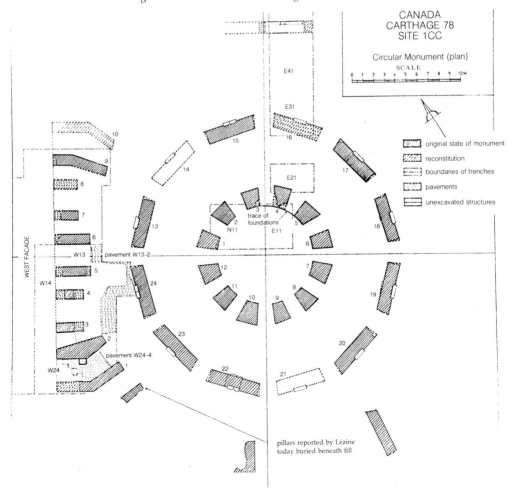

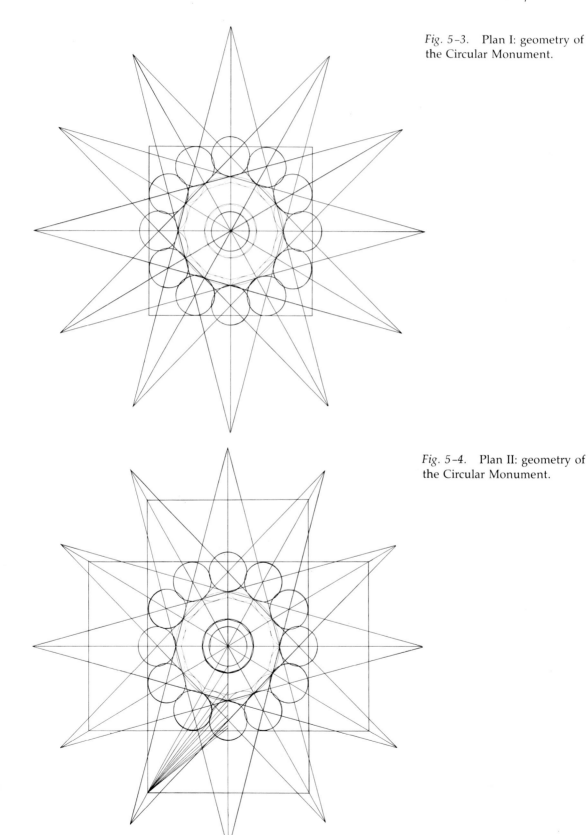

Fig. 5-3. Plan I: geometry of the Circular Monument.

Fig. 5-4. Plan II: geometry of the Circular Monument.

Fig. 6–1. House of the Greek Charioteers, acanthus scroll. (*Courtesy of the Kelsey Museum, University of Michigan.*)

Fig. 6–2. Offering of the Crane, Musée du Bardo. (*Courtesy of Musée du Bardo: after Inventaire.*)

Fig. 6–3. Mosaic of the Months and Seasons, British Museum. (*Courtesy of Trustees of the British Museum.*)

Fig. 6–4. House of the Greek Charioteers, fish mosaic. (*Courtesy of the Kelsey Museum, University of Michigan.*)

Fig. 6–5. Maison de la Cachette de Statues, Triumph of Venus, Musée du Bardo. (*Courtesy of Musée du Bardo; photograph by Katherine Dunbabin.*)

Fig. 6–6. Fish mosaic, British Museum. (*Courtesy of Trustees of the British Museum.*)

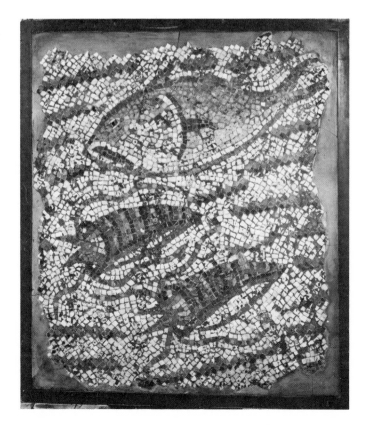

Fig. 6–7.   Hunting scenes, British Museum. (*Courtesy of Trustees of the British Museum.*)